11/95

LOVELAW

ANTHONY CLARE

LOVELAW

LOVE, SEX &
MARRIAGE
AROUND
THE WORLD

BBC PUBLICATIONS

Published by BBC Publications
A division of BBC Enterprises Ltd
35 Marylebone High Street
London W1M 4AA

First published 1986
© Anthony Clare 1986

ISBN 0 563 20467 2 (hardback)
ISBN 0 563 20412 5 (paperback)

Typeset in Melior on linotron by Phoenix Photosetting, Chatham
and printed in England by Mackays of Chatham Ltd

Colour originated and printed by Jolly & Barber Limited, Rugby

CONTENTS

In writing this book I am particularly
grateful to my wife, Jane, for her forbearance
and support, to my constantly encouraging
editor, Sheila Ableman, to the book's designer,
Gillian Shaw, and to the producer of *Lovelaw*,
William Nicholson, who was at all times
the most stimulating of friends. But I am most
indebted to Mukti Jain and Angela Kaye of
Lovelaw who provided the overwhelming bulk of
the data, who shared the fruits of their
labours in Egypt, Kenya, Hungary, Japan,
the US, India and Italy and who commented
constructively on various stages
of the manuscript.

PREFACE

Hardly a day passes without somebody, priest, psychiatrist, politician or pundit, declaring that personal relationships in the modern world are a disaster area. The family is identified as a crumbling institution, permanently under siege, even pronounced by some pessimistic souls as dead. The announcement of this demise, it should be noted, is made with a flourish and a frequency that commentators previously reserved for the obituary notice of the Deity. Hands are wrung with frustration while such phenomena as the permissive society, widespread availability of contraception, the decline in religious belief, the rise in affluence, the influence of advertising and television are individually or collectively blamed for the deterioration in marital and personal relationships and the inexorable rise in statistics testifying to the disintegration.

And the statistics certainly appear impressive. The divorce rate in England and Wales has risen by 600 per cent over the past twenty years. If present trends continue one marriage in three will end in divorce. One child in every eight lives in a one-parent family and one child in every five could well see his or her parents divorce before they reach sixteen. One in four British teenagers is sexually experienced before his or her seventeenth birthday and the number of abortions for fifteen-year-old girls rose from 848 in 1969 to 3058 in 1983. The growing visibility of gay and lesbian relationships and the rising popularity of cohabitation outside marriage suggest to some that not merely the family but marriage itself is doomed.

Across the world, and the traditional divide between the developed and developing parts of it, the crisis seems to loom. Since 1960, the divorce rate has doubled in virtually every European country, and in Barbados it rose tenfold between 1948 and 1975; in Bangladesh and Mexico one in every ten women who has been married has been divorced or separated;

in Colombia the proportion rises to one in five, while in Indonesia it is close to the UK figure at one in three.

In the wash of divorce comes the one-parent family, said to be one of the major causes of poverty in affluent societies and one of the additional social burdens borne by poorer ones. In the UK there were 570,000 such families in 1971, 750,000 in 1976, 920,000 in 1980 and over 1 million at the present time. The overwhelming majority of these families are headed by women, who struggle financially and emotionally to cope in a society which has yet to come to terms with the sheer impact of the trend. In the developing world, marital breakdown coupled with the steady migration of men to the cities mean that the proportion of households headed by women in Peru, Honduras, Venezuela and Cuba is in excess of 20 per cent while in Kenya, Botswana, Ghana and Sierra Leone i⁺ ¹s up to 40 per cent.

As for cohabitation, it has all the appearances of a highly attractive option. The London-based Study Commission on the Family has estimated that whereas only 3 per cent of women who married for the first time in the so-called Swinging Sixties had lived with their husbands before their marriage, this figure had risen to 10 per cent in the early 1970s and to 20 per cent by the end of the decade. In the United States about 4 per cent of all couples were cohabiting in 1981, a 14 per cent increase over the preceding year and a threefold increase since 1970. In Scandinavia, where the tradition of living together for a period before marriage has always been a custom, the practice is now so widespread that terms such as 'premarital sex' and 'living in sin' have a Neanderthal ring to them and the word 'sambo' meaning 'live-in partner' has been coined to take the place of 'my husband' or 'my wife'. With cohabitation has come an increase in the proportion of births outside marriage – 36 per cent in Denmark, 38 per cent in Sweden – but even in countries where cohabitation is nothing like as customary illegitimacy remains high and in Britain one in every six live births is out of wedlock.

While the number of children born outside marriage rises, the number born within remains low or, in some parts of the world, is shrinking below the level necessary for the replacement of the population. In countries such as Norway, West Germany, Hungary and Romania, governments struggle to persuade, bribe, cajole and bully couples into having more children with the same intensity and lack of success that governments in Kenya, Egypt, India and Ghana struggle to persuade couples to have fewer.

Teenage sexuality, abortion, cohabitation, postponed marriage, divorce – such a litany persuades defenders of the traditional model of premarital chastity, marital fidelity and a stable family life that the game is up. And yet, the romantic ideal of love, spectacularly glorified in the United States and exported to the world courtesy of Hollywood and television soap operas, shows little sign of losing its immense appeal. Even in countries such as India, Egypt and Japan where to this day, albeit to varying extents, close relationships between the sexes during adolescence are discouraged, where spouses are selected by parental discussion and decision rather than individual preference and choice, and where love is seen as something that follows rather than precedes marriage, the ideal of romantic love, the model of marriage as a partnership involving companionship and sharing, and the goal of a permanent relationship enduring with fidelity and loyalty 'till death us do part' are steadfastly pursued.

Part of the appeal of the Western-style nuclear family with its emphasis on individual choice and romantic love may lie in the fact that personal and sexual relations within such a model appear to be the concern of the people involved and nobody else – not parents, grandparents, neighbours, the village gossip, the local newspaper or the state itself. In the developed world, personal lives, people insist, are their own business and of no real concern to anyone else. The contrast with other societies is striking, societies in which teenage sexuality is seen to be powerful, unpredictable, dangerous and in need of strict control, and where love is portrayed as an emotion too mercurial and unreliable to be permitted to underpin an institution of such social and political significance as marriage. Having children, being unfaithful, and negotiating separation and divorce are all matters in which the community and the state in such societies expect to have a legitimate and crucial say.

But, of course, even in the developed world love, sex, marriage, family life and divorce are much less our personal business and much more our neighbour's and our community's concern than we care to think. Seemingly private matters such as how we experience and express our sexuality, whether we marry and, if we do, to whom and at what age, whether we have children and, if we do, how many, how they should be reared and who does the rearing, whether we remain faithful to our partners and whether we seek or can obtain a divorce and whether after divorcing we can remarry are all personal decisions embedded in the larger human network of custom, tradition and law.

Every society stipulates the age below which it is an offence to marry. For most countries, the limit is placed in the middle teens, but there are interesting exceptions, most notably China, which has legislated a minimum age of twenty for women and twenty-two for men in an attempt to reduce fertility, while in Southern Asia and sub-Saharan Africa about half of all women aged between fifteen and nineteen are or have been legally married. Many countries, particularly in the developing world, attempt through social policy to reduce the birth rate, while in Romania, a nation alarmed by the inexorable decline in the number of Romanians, formidable restrictions have been placed on the hitherto popular practice of abortion. Every country has laws regulating divorce. In Hungary, for instance, the legal process is easy, financial support is guaranteed to ex-wives and the rate is, not surprisingly perhaps, one of the highest in the world. There are even laws affecting the sex roles within marriage, the most notable being those enacted by Sweden where the fathers and the mothers of children under eight years of age are entitled to reduce their work input to a six-hour day.

But if our love-lives are significantly affected or even regulated by a complex mixture of personal choice, parental influence, social custom and legally-enacted statutes, why cannot we make a better fist of it all? Of course, it is possible that things are better than we think they are, that the Jeremiahs and the Cassandras warning of the imminent collapse of family life are just reading the entrails the wrong way up. Perhaps those parts of the developing world anxiously striving to imitate our social mores perceive an inherent value in our seeming chaos which escapes the critics. Personally, as a man, a husband, a father of a large family, and a psychiatrist, I find myself badgered by the headlines and the news flashes concerning illegitimacy, abortion, child abuse, divorce and single-parenthood into believing that the foundations are indeed giving way. My teenage children seem at times to be inordinately pressurised into premature sexual activity by persistent media messages glamorising teenage independence and romantic experience. My wife is buffeted and torn by societal values which emphatically idealise a hopelessly serene and romantic notion of motherhood while simultaneously highlighting the emotional and economic cost of child-bearing and its negative impact on career choice and personal satisfaction. Together we struggle to maintain and develop our personal relationship amidst the deafening noise of marriages collapsing around us. And in my psychiatric clinic I find doubts and uncertainties reflected in the stresses and strains of my patients as they battle to reconcile the often irreconcilable aspirations of self-fulfilment and enduring personal relationships.

In the midst of such confusions, I was telephoned two years ago by Sheila Ableman, a publishing editor with the BBC, and William Nicholson, a television producer with the same corporation. Nicholson, I learned, was about to commence filming a series of seven 50-minute programmes under the title *Lovelaw*, designed to examine how people of widely differing cultural backgrounds regulate the universal processes of falling in love, choosing a spouse, sustaining a marriage, bearing children and contemplating a divorce. The series was to be filmed in seven countries – India, Kenya, Egypt, Hungary, Japan, the United States and Italy – and in each country filming would focus on a single, urban community. Each film would concentrate on a specific issue such as the customs and controls surrounding young love, the choosing of a spouse, the obtaining of a divorce. What Ableman and Nicholson invited me to do was to look at all the filmed material – not just the material to be included in the programmes – sit in on the extensive briefing and debriefing sessions attended by Nicholson and his colleagues before they set off for and after they had returned from locations, familiarise myself with the voluminous background literature accumulated throughout the course of the programme-making and provided by the expert advisers selected in each of the countries involved, and then write a book based on but not necessarily identical to the *Lovelaw* series.

Thus did this book evolve. In common with, I suspect, the overwhelming majority of the viewers of the series, my knowledge of and familiarity with several of the seven countries involved is slight. I have looked at their customs, values and traditions as they have been portrayed on the small screen and I have looked at them through the eyes of a middle-class Westerner, fascinated by such seemingly anachronistic practices as arranged marriage and polygamy, bride-price and 'love hotels', and curious to know the advantages and disadvantages of what appear to be very different answers to the universal problems of love, marriage, procreation and separation.

In some ways, the book has stayed close to the television series, concentrating in the main on those countries in which filming occurred. However, at times direct comparisons are made with life in Britain and at times material and information from other countries are assessed. I ought to say at this point that the television series restricts its interest to heterosexual relationships. Homosexual relationships require more detailed discussion and consideration than time and space allowed. Also, that throughout the book, characters are addressed and titled as they would be in their countries of origin.

In the final chapter, after considering such issues as young love, the choice of spouse, the limits of fidelity and problems of divorce, I raise the question as to whether we can usefully derive any insights of value from the ways in which people regulate their personal lives in societies very different from our own. Our own rules, laws, customs and traditions do not appear to be working or at least are not working very well; what, if anything, have other societies and cultures to teach us? And if, as appears to be the case, all societies at the end of the twentieth century are in a state of flux and confusion, can we detect any basic ground rules, any stable signposts indicating the most fruitful ways forward to the elusive goal of successful, harmonious, durable human relationships?

Anthony Clare, 1986

1 YOUNG LOVE

Love, or so it is said, makes the world go around. It strikes across a crowded room, sweeps us off our feet, makes fools rush in where the angels fear to tread. Love is variously portrayed as a force, a fuel, an elixir, a drug, a snare, a biological trick to ensure the survival of the species, a gift from God to remind man of the divine life. Western culture is awash in romantic love and is distinct in stressing love *before* marriage and in emphasising the process of 'falling in love' as the necessary prelude to choosing a spouse, forming as permanent relationship and having children. Physical attractiveness, emotional compatibility and the ability to share specific roles are amongst the prized qualities sought in a potential spouse and the freedom to choose is itself highly valued. Indeed, such a freedom is seen to be the high-water mark of a mature society and an indicator of the demise of feudal conceptions of marriage and the family and of parental domination and control.

Romantic love is big business. The best-known international publisher of romantic fiction is the British publishing firm of Mills & Boon with 1500 titles on their list, each of which sells between 80,000 and 100,000 copies. The books have been translated into Spanish, French, Dutch, German and even Bahasa Indonesia. The mass-marketing of romance through such fiction and through television soap operas has drawn the fire of feminists who lament the stereotyped sex roles they appear to endorse. In the words of Barbara Cartland, 'All my heroines are good, pure and very, very womanly, tender and sweet. All my heroes are sporting and very, very dominating, but honourable, because that is what a woman wants.'

The world's appetite for film romance is expanding too. An estimated 71 per cent of television programmes in the developing countries are imports from the rich world. Women's magazines and advertising add the finishing touches, 'entangling the tender allure of romantic love,' as Debbie Taylor[1] somewhat pungently puts it, 'inextricably with the athletic exotica of penetrative sex and the mundane demands of a woman's domestic duties.'

Whatever we think about the link between romantic love and a particular sex role, what cannot be doubted is that romantic love with its endorsement of love as the basis of marriage has weakened direct parental control over the process of choosing a spouse. Parents in Western societies cannot control with whom their child will fall in love, save indirectly by bringing up the child to be more compatible with people who hold certain values and come from certain backgrounds.

But should romantic or teenage love be controlled? In other societies, particularly in the East, romantic love is recognised for the passion it is and is subjected to varying degrees of control. Such love is seen to follow rather than to precede the choice of spouse in the arranged marriage model of India and Japan. Romantic love, in such societies, is seen to be an emotional, physiological urge; exciting but unreliable as the basis for the complicated parental, family, social and communal process which is the choice of a spouse and the foundation of a new family unit.

The need for control would appear to derive from the understandable anxiety that romantic love, occurring as it usually does first in adolescence, leads to premarital sexual intercourse which in turn can lead either to teenage pregnancy, marriage or both. These outcomes appear equally disastrous. Teenage marriage is astonishingly brittle, particularly if a pregnancy is involved – approximately 20 per cent of such marriages in the UK are dissolved within two years of having been contracted, while teenage pregnancy is in many instances a social disaster. At the present time, pregnancy in adolescence accounts for about 10 to 15 per cent of births worldwide but this is certainly an underestimate since many teenage pregnancies are terminated by legal or illegal abortion. Because couples in the developing world marry earlier, most teenage pregnancy is within marriage, whereas in developed countries, with later average ages of marriage, more teenage pregnancies occur outside marriage. In 1979, for example, almost two of every three live births to US teenagers were to unwed mothers. A World

Bank report in 1984 anticipated that as the age of marriage rises and urbanisation loosens traditional social restraints on sexual activity, the incidence of premarital teenage pregnancy would increase in the developing world.

Teenage pregnancy poses well-known and less well-known hazards. In developed as well as developing countries, children of teenage mothers are more likely to be premature, have low birth weight and have a greater risk of death during childbirth. Pregnancy and childbirth interrupt the educational progress and affect the career prospects of teenage mothers as they frequently fail to complete their education. The children of adolescent mothers are also at a disadvantage. Teenage couples are likely to have fewer economic assets than somewhat older couples, and single teenage mothers have even less. In the developing world, the plight of such children and mothers can be stark. In Brazil, for example, an estimated 16 million children or one-third of its youth have young mothers who are unwed or who are in unstable relationships. In the developed world, children of young mothers are likely to spend a considerable part of their childhood in single-parent households and in turn are more likely to have children themselves when still adolescents.

While every society attempts to control teenage sexuality in order to avoid pregnancy, abortion and parenthood, there are considerable variations in approach. These range from parts of

TEENAGE ABORTIONS IN EUROPE									
Country	BULGARIA	DENMARK	ENGLAND & WALES	FINLAND	EAST GERMANY	NORWAY	POLAND	SWEDEN	YUGOSLAVIA
Year	77	78	76	75	76	76	78	76	76
% of women having abortions who are teenagers	17	18	24	18	12	5	6	18	8

> *Recognising that pregnancy occurring in adolescent girls, whether married or unmarried, has adverse effects on the morbidity and mortality of both mother and child, Governments are urged to develop policies to encourage delay in the commencement of childbearing. Governments should make efforts to raise the age of entry into marriage in countries in which this age is still quite low. Attention should also be given to ensuring that adolescents, both girls and boys, receive adequate information and education.[2]*
>
> *United Nations Report, Nairobi, 1985*

India, where strict segregation of the adolescent sexes is enforced and where a young man often only sees his intended wife just before he marries her, and talks to her only after, to California, where young people have the highest degree of mobility and freedom in the world and where parental control is reduced to declaring, with varying degrees of firmness or feebleness, that curfew is midnight and if junior is not back before then the car will be impounded.

At the local high school in the small northern Californian town of Los Gatos *Lovelaw* filmed teenagers tumbling out of school, jumping into their cars in the car park and roaring off down Main Street to indulge in a spot of 'cruising', an activity which involves much waving at each other, hilarity and shouted conversation, and the arrangement of 'dates' for later that evening. On the school sports field, fresh-faced, loose-limbed adolescent girls rehearsed their sexy, lithe cheer-leader routines for Saturday's football game, while on the school stage a couple went through a scene from *Romeo and Juliet*. But a few additional touches remind us that this is California, a state with one of the highest teenage pregnancy and abortion rates in the world. Indeed in nearby San José, there is even a high school which specifically caters for pregnant schoolgirls and schoolgirl mothers. The school has a crèche where young mothers take their babies on their way to class. Elsewhere pregnant schoolgirls are being trained in child care.

The juxtaposition of pregnancy and high school reflects the conflict in US society between a desire to give adolescents considerable freedom and high expectations concerning education and career. The fundamental problem is that in a society where children mature earlier than ever (the average Los Gatos

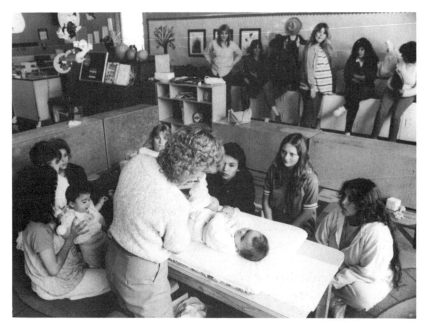

A special school for schoolgirl mothers in San José, California. Here the girls can continue their schooling as well as having crèche facilities and advice on baby care

schoolgirl first menstruates before her twelfth birthday) they are exposed to an atmosphere lush in romanticism, eroticism and sexuality with few parental controls and fewer still established social customs to help them cope. What seems to be the situation, if the authors of a recent report[3] from the Alan Guttmacher Institute in New York are correct, is that American teenagers have inherited the worst of all possible worlds,

> Movies, music, radio and TV tell them that sex is romantic, exciting, titillating; premarital sex and cohabitation are visible ways of life among the adults they see and hear about; their own parents or their parents' friends are likely to be divorced or separated but involved in sexual relationships. Yet at the same time, young people get the message good girls say no. Almost nothing that they see or hear about sex informs them about contraception or the importance of avoiding pregnancy. For example, they are more likely to hear about abortions than about contraception on the daily TV soap opera.

As a result, every year ninety-six teenagers in every 1000 become pregnant in the US compared with forty-five per 1000 in England and Wales, Canada and France, and thirty-five per

1000 in Sweden and fourteen per 1000 in the Netherlands. Such a high rate of pregnancy cannot be explained merely by assuming that more US teenagers engage in sexual activity than teenagers elsewhere in the West. In most European countries, the median age at first coitus is seventeen to eighteen years for boys and about nineteen for girls, not significantly higher than in the US. Indeed, in Sweden adolescents appear even more sexually active than their American counterparts yet their rates of pregnancy and abortion are very much lower. By the age of sixteen approximately 33 per cent of Swedish girls have had intercourse and by the age of eighteen 80 per cent have done so.

Sweden, in company with other Scandinavian countries, takes a pragmatic view of adolescent sexuality and lays considerable emphasis on the hazards of unwanted pregnancies and the need for sex education and contraception. The American response, in contrast, is particularly ambiguous and ambivalent. As Hannah Kennedy, a teacher at Broadway High School for pregnant schoolgirls in San José, makes plain, while it is the norm amongst Californian teenagers to have sex, their parents prefer not to talk to them about it because they do not want to appear to condone it. The young American teenager has been given the freedom to experiment sexually but basic attitudes of the culture have failed to change accordingly. Teenagers interviewed at Los Gatos admitted that the stereotypes of the sexually experienced young male as an admired stud and of the sexually experienced young female as a 'slag' or prostitute still persist – and this in a society where *both* sexes are under strong external societal and peer pressures to become sexually active. Likewise, few young men take any

AGE OF BRITISH RESPONDENTS AT FIRST COITUS*	
Under 16	5%
16–17	18%
18–19	22%
20–21	19%
22–24	13%
25+	7%
Still a virgin	4%
Refused to say	12%

BASE: ALL WOMEN AGED 18+   *MORI POLL 1984

interest in contraception, while young women who do leave themselves open to the accusation of being sexually voracious or promiscuous.

Viewed from the perspective of a society which takes a much more controlling view of teenage love, the Californian state of affairs looks somewhat unappealing. In India, over 60 per cent of women before marriage have no knowledge whatsoever of sex, according to two commentators, Drs Girija Khanna and Marlamma Verghese, writing in the magazine *Indian Women Today*. In contrast, by the time they reach matrimony 78 per cent of American men and over 50 per cent of American women are no longer virgins.

Lovelaw filmed young Indian teenagers in the cities of Madras and Madurai in the southern Indian state of Tamil Nadu. The state is comparable in size to England and the population is 90 per cent Hindu. The Tamils regard themselves as the most pure and true Indians, least affected by the invasion of other cultures. Madras, the state capital, is a cosmopolitan city of about 5 million with a large textile manufacturing industry. It is also the centre of India's film industry, which in terms of the number of movies produced is the biggest in the world. Madras is not as overcrowded or as densely populated as Bombay or Calcutta and is generally regarded as a more relaxed and safer city than most cities of its size.

On the streets of Madras, young people of both sexes move quite freely but closer inspection reveals that girls are with girls and boys with boys. In such a carefully organised and structured society, conversation between a teenage boy and girl would be regarded as tantamount to a proposal of marriage. Yet, on many of the hoardings and billboards in the city can be seen advertisements for the romantic films beloved by the 100 million Indians who go to the cinema every week and who follow avidly the public and personal lives of the film stars.

Most Indian film-makers admit that the romantic stories, with their themes of forbidden love, adultery and divorce, are pure fantasy and bear no relation to what goes on in the real life of most Indians. On the set of a Tamil movie being shot in Madras, *Lovelaw* watched as the two stars embraced and kissed – almost. The male lead, Suman, a famous south Indian film star, admitted that this is pure fantasy too. In reality it is impossible for him to be alone with an unmarried girl, let alone touch her. Whatever his own wishes, and he is somewhat envious of the greater freedom in this matter in the West, it would be the ruin of the girl's reputation. Indeed, even on celluloid, the relationship between the sexes is strictly regulated – no suggestion of love-making is permitted but intense, romantic involvement is suggested by songs, dances and dream-like sequences which may end in an embrace.

Of course, the situation is slowly changing and a greater degree of mixing between adolescents of both sexes is underway in Madras and neighbouring Madurai. Madurai, with a population of almost 1 million, is a somewhat more conservative and provincial city than Madras – a hot, dusty, overgrown village rather than a city, with narrow streets crowded with bullocks and bicycles. It is famous for its huge Meenakshi Temple, which resembles a multicoloured, multi-towered religious department store around which all life appears to revolve. Less influenced by other than traditional Hindu culture, Madurai society strictly regulates such contact as young Indians have with members of the opposite sex. In effect, they only meet when there is a clear prospect of marriage. The choice of a marriage partner is itself scrupulously controlled and involves the active participation of the two families. Casual conversation between a boy and a girl could well prejudice the girl's chances by earning her the reputation of being cheap or available. Indians recognise, of course, that there is attraction between the sexes in adolescence but a clear distinction is drawn between such attraction and the concept of love. Love comes after marriage and not before. In the words of one Indian interviewed about the impact of an arranged marriage, 'When we marry somebody our parents choose for us, we are just eliminating the trial and error.'

The Western-style roundabout of sexual exploration and choice, which has been termed the 'leap of faith' by the American sociologist, Ira Reiss, is seen as wildly irresponsible.

Marriage in traditional India involves issues of caste, dowry, the impact on the fortunes and prospects of the remaining unmarried sons and daughters of the families concerned and the fact that the new wife is expected to move in with her husband's family. It cannot depend on the two central participants

> *The first question is what do we mean by love? What our parents say about love is that you marry and you love not only your wife but your children, your neighbours and everything. However, the only other things that speak to us about love are books and films. But the books and the films do not give any real idea about love or what happens after you love someone and get married. We have experienced arranged marriages and we have seen that they go well. But those couples who marry after dating and all those things, mostly they go away from the parents and then break up. And so we say, if you go away from your parents and then marry you will have to bear all alone your sufferings but otherwise you will have your parents, your brothers and sisters and you will have moral support. We are attached to this side of marriage.*
>
> Young Indian student
> on love and marriage

making their own choice on a romantic and emotional basis. Not surprisingly, the southern Indian equivalent of the Californian 'date' is a somewhat more formal process, with intimidating implications. Back in Madurai *Lovelaw* filmed a young man combing his hair and powdering his cheeks, while further down the street in her own home a young woman is being beautified by her sisters. This is the real Indian world and not the celluloid fantasy and a young man is about to meet his future wife for the very first time. In modern India there are few truly 'blind' marriages now. Instead, there is what is called the 'girl-seeing ceremony'. The young man and his entire family proceed down the street to the young woman's house where they are met by her family. While she waits in a side room, the young man is seated on a chair and everyone else sits on the floor. The young woman is sent for, kneels and bows before the young man, and then leaves. The whole procedure rarely takes longer than five minutes. But she has managed to peep at him and he at her. Both can now say yes or no to the proposed match.

Young Indians of both sexes are well aware of the restrictions on their lives compared with the West. To a degree they are envious of their contemporaries in Los Gatos but they also believe that were they to enjoy such freedom their society would disintegrate. They are right – Indian society as it is today would collapse, as societies such as Kenya show signs of doing as a consequence of too rapid a transition. The Indian students

The price of romantic love is high in India. When Amalraj and Harini eloped six years ago, they were both rejected by their families. They are likely to remain isolated for the rest of their lives

interviewed by *Lovelaw* believed in general that the only way to stand any chance of being satisfied with their partner in real life is to have known only one member of the opposite sex outside the family.

The arranged marriage underpins and interlocks with many aspects of traditional Indian life and most particularly the supportive infrastructure provided by the extended family. The sexual freedom of American adolescents suggests to Indian observers not simply promiscuity but a fearful and isolating independence. Indian families meet often, regularly sitting down to share a family meal. Grandparents are there to care for grandchildren. There is always an aunt, a sister, a cousin to look after the smallest children. In Western societies such as California, the tradition of big family groups has evaporated and mothers without family support and living in marked social isolation have become a major social problem.

In other societies, a rapid transition from the traditional, controlled model of adolescent sexuality to the permissive Western model can have a profoundly disruptive effect. In Africa, Kenya is typical of a modern Third World country that has made a rapid but socially turbulent change from a traditional agrarian way of life to Western-style industrialisation. After 1964, in the first flush of independence, the economy boomed and education spread. By 1975, primary school fees having been abolished by Jomo Kenyatta, 92 per cent of all school-age children were at school. Education was quickly seen as the most important and effective way of obtaining a good job and earning good money.

The economic recession coupled with a persistently high birth rate leading to one of the youngest populations in the world have severely impeded Kenya's progress. Large numbers of school-leavers, particularly girls, are finding it increasingly difficult to obtain employment. Where once Kenya was a fiercely patriarchal society with many, though not all, men heading large, polygamous families, rapid urbanisation has led to the accumulation of young men in urban areas often hundreds of miles away from wives and families. To these same urban areas have come many young, unemployed, unmarried, educated women. These social changes have been accompanied by a breakdown in the sexual mores and constraints of traditional Kenya.

At the Alliance High School in Nairobi, the prestige academy

> Why do I describe them as social slaves, those young girls who have succumbed to the temptation to give sexual favours to the person who has money in order to survive and in order for their babies to survive? These are the reasons: there is need for money, for yourself and for your child. There is a need for shelter, a need for clothing. Where is it going to come from? Now those things are going to come from, again, men with money. I'll keep calling them men with money so that you understand who I'm talking about. Men with money are therefore going to dictate to you because it is said he who pays the piper calls the tune. And a person who has the money now, who is paying for that baby, paying for the accommodation, paying for the clothes, what he says is what you are going to have to do and your views are not invited; because you have lost any right to choose your man. You cannot any more.[4]
>
> Dr Samuel Gatere

of the nation's youth, the assembly hall is packed with senior students of both sexes to hear a lecture by the psychiatrist, Dr Samuel Gatere. His message is starkly simple: the senior girls must consider themselves at war, a war between the sexes, in which young men seek to enslave and corrupt them. The crisis that has hit Kenya means that the economy has become cash-based, all the power is now in the hands of the men and many women can only survive by selling themselves. The girls have a duty to resist. The situation is desperate. Tribal culture has collapsed and the Western substitute is ineffective. Nearly one in five Kenyan girls becomes pregnant while still at school (close to the rate at Los Gatos). There is widespread failure to use contraceptives. A social disintegration is underway.

And where, amidst this bleak vision of modern Kenya, is love? 'No Romance without Finance' sings a Nairobi pop group, yet to judge by the bestselling magazine in the country, *True Love*, love is everywhere and all you need. The magazine, the usual mix of romantic fiction, agony column, pop star pull-outs and advertisements for beauty aids and cosmetics, unabashedly fosters the notion of romantic love – all-powerful, all-enduring, all-faithful. Yet Kenyan teenagers appear remarkably

Opposite and above. *Nairobi teenagers reading the popular magazine* True
Love. *They find that the sentiments expressed in it do not conform with real
life in Kenya*

cynical about such notions. 'Men are liars,' says one young
Kenyan girl when asked her views on love. 'Only about one in a
hundred is capable of falling in love while the rest cheat and
indulge in many affairs.' There is a familiar claim that men and
women differ in relation to their emotional needs. 'You can find
a girl who has committed her whole life, her whole love to just
one person,' adds the Kenyan teenager, 'but there is hardly a
man who really has the urge to have one girlfriend.' Boys expect
girls to sleep with them and their standing among their peers is
judged by the success with which they persuade many to do so.
But parents are strict and girls are ill-prepared for the double
standards concerning sexual experience that govern adolescent
behaviour.

True Love attempts to calm the situation. It runs a cartoon
story in which the girl finds her boyfriend with other girls, a not
unfamiliar Kenyan experience. Hurt and bewildered, she
leaves him. The happy ending is contrived by way of the revelation that the other girls were really the boyfriend's sisters! True
love blossoms again.

Shown this romantic story, teenage Kenyan girls and boys
find it ridiculous. To the Western observer, however, they

appear caught in a culture clash. The girls appear to be influenced by Western ideas of romance, monogamy, fidelity and the nuclear family with its emphasis on sharing, companionship and communication between the partners. This may well in part reflect the Family Life programmes that are beginning to be taught in schools and which stress a somewhat idealised version of the Western family. The young Kenyan males, on the other hand, seem much less influenced by such modern notions. They, in their attitudes towards women, pride, sexual status and peer approval, seem more in tune with their traditional elders, many of whom lived in a polygamous culture. The difference, however, is that whatever its disadvantages the system of polygamy enjoined the participating men with the responsibility of looking after, caring for and protecting their womenfolk. Today, young Kenyan men seem very much more cavalier about what happens to the young women with whom they have casual sexual contact.

In one of Nairobi's many smart and fashionable discos, *Lovelaw* interviewed a pretty young woman called Fatuma Mombi. Love is one commodity that poor Mombie (as she is known) can no longer afford. Her story is sadly a typical one. At fifteen and when still at school, little Mombie fell in love with an eighteen-year-old boy at the same school. After six months, her boyfriend insisted on sex and subsequently she became pregnant. Forced to leave school and deserted by her boyfriend, Mombie lived with her mother until the birth of her child. While her mother looked after the child, Mombie learned shorthand and obtained a job as a secretary in Nairobi. But her attempt to establish her own financial independence was subverted by yet another man who appeared to take pity on her, took her off to another town, mistreated her, refused to allow her to take contraceptive measures and made her pregnant. Finally, she returned to her mother and gave birth to twin daughters. By now, her mother was unable to cope financially and Mombie was forced to find money to enable herself and her daughters to survive. Well-nigh unemployable in a city where even skilled labour is cheap and plentiful, Mombie was forced to join the numerous young prostitutes servicing the foreign tourists thronging the luxury hotels that have sprung up in downtown Nairobi.

So now, each evening, Mombie washes her two daughters,

Mombie and her twin daughters outside their Nairobi flat. Like many Kenyan women who cannot find employment Mombie works as a prostitute in the tourist hotels

feeds them, puts them to bed, locks them inside her tiny apartment and sets off for one of the hotels. Her dream is that she will meet some wealthy tourist, an American perhaps or a Swede, who will whisk her away. Her nightmare is that her daughters will succumb to the new, permissive atmosphere of urban Kenya and end up replicating her own predicament.

Between traditional India, struggling to maintain its structured stance towards love, sex and marriage, and turbulent Kenya, rapidly adopting Western attitudes and aspirations while struggling with its well-established stereotypes of male and female sexuality, lies modern Japan, affluent, industrialised and thriving. Youth culture in Japan, particularly in the cities, appears remarkably Westernised with its predilection for rock music and Western styles of dress and personal adornment. The popular reading material is the cartoon romance book with its plethora of love stories in which all the characters have Western appearances and express Western notions of romantic love and desire.

The reality, Japanese teenagers insist, is somewhat different. In modern Japan, there is still much less contact between young boys and girls than in the West. Many work hard at college, live

> *I always tell them when they ask, 'Mama, where are you going?' that I'm going upstairs to watch TV, or to a friend's or sometimes I tell them I'm going out for a disco. Sometimes they wonder. They ask me, 'Mama, do you have to go for a disco every night?' I'll tell them, 'Yes. You sleep. You are small, tomorrow you are going to school.' And then they sleep. They have no idea where I go because I don't bring men home. I don't like them to have that idea. I don't like them to live a life like me. I try very hard to make sure they get everything, let's say for schooling especially the uniform, or food. I make sure that they don't starve or they don't miss anything so that they continue with their schooling. I try very hard to teach them at home every time when they come out from school because I collect them at 12.30. When I bring them they find food ready. I feed them. They remove their uniform. We go on with what they've been doing at school so I try and keep them busy and hope they will be able to live a better life than me.*
>
> Mombie, twenty-four-year-old single
> mother of three

at home, associate sex with a very special, highly romanticised love and eschew promiscuity. Most of the obsession with sex visible in Japanese society at the present time, they insist, arises from their parents' generation which had been so repressed sexually that it over-reacted when it encountered post-war freedom.

Nevertheless, the trends identified in urban Kenya can be seen here too. Attitudes towards premarital sex have rapidly changed; in a recent poll, 70 per cent of women and 80 per cent of men aged between twenty and twenty-four years believed that sex before marriage is acceptable between those who love each other. This is in a country where, until quite recently, daughters were taught, 'You're a girl, you must cover your mouth when you smile.' As the ideal of love more closely approximates to Western values, so Japan is experiencing an increase in familiar Western problems. The frequency of abortions has doubled among teenage Japanese girls in the past ten years. Divorce steadily rises – the rate is now close to that of West Germany and France though still only half the British rate and a quarter of that of the US.

Looked at more closely, the norms and ideals of the average young Japanese couple reflect the confusion of values. Along the riverbank of the beautiful city of Kyoto can be seen

numerous young couples in love. One such pair, Kayou Takeu-
chi and Yoshitaka Tanino, are both twenty years old although
they met while still at school. They live with their parents and
Kayou imposes a personal curfew on herself of 10 pm each
night. Rarely, about once every six months, she stays out later.
They admit to being very much in love, confessing to a preoccupation with each other when apart, intense joy and satisfaction
when together. They drive, go to the cinema, spend about 80 per
cent of their available money sampling the many excellent restaurants of their city. Occasionally, but unknown to their
parents, they sleep together, by day, in one of the 35,000 'love
hotels' that are a feature of Japan. These are hotels where rooms
can be hired by the hour. They have a long tradition in a country
where red-light districts were once referred to as 'flower-and-
willow worlds'.

In general, however, the relationship between Kayou and
Yoshitaka is a serious one, a relationship of self-discipline,
obedience to parents and solemn expectations concerning the
future. Love, while enjoyable and sought after, must not be
allowed to interfere with more important matters, in particular
with Yoshitaka's studies and his prospects of a good job. While
marriage is a possibility, Kayou's parents are against it. Her
father, a doctor, is hoping that she will marry a potential partner
for the family practice. It is, after all, a country with a strong
tradition of arranged marriages. Anyway, both Kayou and
Yoshitaka have cars, money, are studying hard and are
extremely hard-headed about this thing called love. Love is not
something for which one is going to make too many sacrifices.
Love sacrifices are for the stage of the Takarazuka Theatre.

This enormously popular institution appears to satisfy the
strong Japanese desire to fantasise about passionate emotion
while in reality keeping it under firm control. Onstage at the
theatre, a handsome young man sings a tragic love song from its
latest offering, a musical version of *A Tale of Two Cities*. The
theatre makes a speciality of intense, romantic melodramas
borrowed from the West. Around the walls are colourful pos-
ters relating to previous productions, including such smash
hits as *Napoleon and Josephine* and *Gone with the Wind*. The
curiosity is that the young man singing the love song onstage
and the dashingly handsome Rhett Butler gazing down from the

> In Japan, although there have been rapid changes with regard to
> love since the Second World War, basically love between a man
> and a woman has not changed. That is to say, it is still based on
> the pre-war idea that 'when boys and girls reach seven years of
> age they should not mix'. A Japanese does not express his feelings
> immediately on falling in love, in contrast to the Westerner who
> will express his or her feelings immediately verbally. However, in
> Japan reading another's thoughts was and is necessary. In the
> olden days we expected others to feel and read our thoughts
> without our telling them everything. We believed this was more
> refined. I think the Takarazuka opera follows this idea. There are
> few love scenes where a man and a woman meet and embrace
> each other. The man and the woman on the stage understand this
> and let their feelings be known to each other while keeping a
> certain distance. This the audience sees and understands all too
> well.
>
> Mr Ohta, Director of the
> Takarazuka Theatre's production of
> A Tale of Two Cities

poster in the foyer are not men at all but women; all the 'actors'
in this theatre are in fact female and the most famous of them –
and many of them are household names in Japan – are the
actresses who specialise in male hero roles.

The writer and director of the musical, A Tale of Two Cities,
Mr Ohta, explains the popularity of romantic drama and musi-
cals in Japan. Takarazuka offers romantic love without sex. All
the productions are of doomed love. The present production,
after all, features a hero who loves in vain and with such nobi-
lity that he gives up his life for it. This is a particularly Japanese
preoccupation, the idea of love as an intense feeling which if
yielded up to can lead to destruction. Powerful love is inextricably bound up with self-sacrifice and self-sacrifice invariably
involves death.

It is an intriguing split and one which in a later chapter
(Chapter 5) is reflected again in the way in which contemporary
Japanese values separate marital and family love from sexual
feelings. The former, like romantic love, are important, significant, bound up with duty and responsibility. Sex, however, is
stripped of its power and transformed into a recreation, a
pastime, a trivial distraction, an escape.

For all the apparent complexity with which various societies construct their laws and customs for the regulation of love, and in particular young love, the number of ways whereby it might be disciplined and kept in check are actually rather limited. Many Latin American societies place their faith in a form of chaperonage but are under siege from the pervasive American emphasis on teenage freedom, independence and mobility. India struggles to isolate the sexes premaritally and maintains this strategy by emphasising the wider familial, social and communal benefits of the arranged marriage. Japan and the United States, in common with most other affluent and developed societies, rely on a variable mixture of indirect parental controls and peer pressures. But such strategies and controls appear increasingly inadequate in the face of an emphasis on love-based relationships strengthened by the increased freedom of young people and the weakening of duty-based rela-

A poster of the Takarazuka Theatre production of Gone with the Wind

tionships by economic independence and geographical distance.

So how is young love to be regulated? There are signs, particularly in Scandinavia, of the evolution of a less ambivalent attitude towards teenage sexuality and love. Systematic sex education, a pragmatic approach towards contraception and, by means of cohabitation, a socially accepted method of postponing marriage and child-bearing may be leading to the emergence of a cluster of customs, controls and pressures appropriate to the times. (See Chapter 7.)

In Britain, however, we shirk from the Scandinavian solution. The issue of teenage sexuality still disturbs and confuses. Sex education and the provision of contraception are seen by many as little more than an invitation to adolescents to experiment sexually. Meanwhile Britain pays a price, similar to though still less than the equivalent American price, of high teenage pregnancy rates, high rates of illegitimacy and high teenage abortion rates. Moralists and critics of the 'permissive society' hanker for the time when adolescents preserved their virginity, chastity was a virtue and the most popular contraceptive was 'No'. But there is hardly a society which shows much sign of turning the clock back. The one striking exception is Ireland, where the low proportion of births recorded to unmarried women, together with the tiny proportion of marriages ending in divorce and the apparently small numbers living in consensual unions, presents a marked contrast with the situation in the rest of Europe. However, the Irish demographer, Brendan Walsh, has recently observed of Irish trends,

> It is a safe prediction that change will continue and possibly accelerate in all these areas, bringing Irish patterns of behaviour more closely into line with those found elsewhere in Western Europe.[5]

Slowly all parts of the world are being 'brought into line'. One effect, however, is the shared anxiety that the powerful combination of adolescent sexuality and teenage freedom will lead to an inexorable rise in the already high rates of illegitimacy, teenage abortions and, as we will see later, teenage marriage. The challenge is as clear as it is difficult to meet: how to reconcile teenage personal freedom with appropriate sexual responsibility, how to ensure that when eventually individuals opt to marry their choice, in so far as it is possible, is the right choice.

2   THE RIGHT CHOICE

Current discussions about marriage tend to focus on the increase in the rate of marital breakdown. What is often ignored is the fact that marriage as an institution has never been so popular. The proportion of eligible persons marrying has steadily increased during the course of the twentieth century. In mid-Victorian England, by contrast, almost one-third of women remained unmarried. In 1911, of every 1000 women aged between twenty and forty, just over half were married. In 1931, the figure was still less than 60 per cent. By 1961 it had reached 80 per cent. And while the 1970s have seen a slight downturn in the marriage rate, the fact remains that on the basis of 1976 marriage patterns less than 8 per cent of women and 14 per cent of men will remain unmarried throughout their lives. In the United States, despite the increase in cohabitation outside marriage, marriage itself endures as a highly prized state. By their early thirties over 90 per cent of Americans have married and only about 6 per cent of men and 4 per cent of women reach their fifties still single.

The explanation for the slight decline in the UK marriage rate may reflect a growing disillusion with marriage as an institution. On the other hand, it may merely be a consequence of the fact that the numerical balance between the sexes is changing. There is a relative scarcity of marriageable women which is growing. In addition, the long-term trend towards earlier marriage has gone into reverse. People decide not so much whether or not to marry as when – and in the 1980s more are postponing marriage until later.

Lesley Rimmer, Deputy Director of the Family Policy Studies Centre in London, reviewing marriage trends in the United Kingdom, believes that the falling rate of marriage can largely be explained by this changed timing of marriage and suspects that 'it is premature to regard the decline in marriage rates in the

1970s as signifying "the end of marriage".' A rise or fall in the proportions of men and women marrying at early ages is often compensated for by changes later on, and at the present time it is hard to tell whether the recent decline in early marriage will be compensated for by a rise in the proportions marrying later on.

One of the most cherished assumptions of post-war Western life is that everyone should be perfectly free to marry whomsoever he or she wishes. Western marriage, ideally at any rate, is the consequence of a love match. This is not to suggest that many a marriage is not influenced by considerations of social class, educational attainment, family acceptability and parental consent. Many are, of course, but the ideal that is laid out before society is of two people romantically attracted to each other, seeking and establishing strong emotional bonds, swearing mutual fidelity until death and freely entering into the marital state. This freedom is borne out by the sharp fall in the number of so-called 'shot-gun marriages'. The number of births conceived prior to and subsequently born within marriage in the UK has dramatically fallen during the 1970s – by over 50 per cent between 1971 and 1977 alone.

Contributory factors to this fall doubtless include the greater availability and variety of contraception and the legalisation of abortion. It would appear that when a child is conceived outside marriage in contemporary Britain, women are more likely to have an abortion or bear an illegitimate child than they are to marry in order to legitimise their offspring. In 1981, 75 per cent of teenage pregnancies occurred outside marriage but only 19 per cent resulted in marriage. Half the remainder were terminated by abortion and in the remaining cases the mothers had their babies without marrying. The registration of many illegitimate babies in both their parents' names suggests that cohabitation between the parents may have been involved, or at least the existence of a positive and mutually supportive relationship. This process of destigmatising illegitimacy has gone furthest in Sweden where today married and unmarried couples have in most cases equal status before the law. Swedish legislation since the late 1960s has been based on the view that the emotional needs of children can be satisfied outside orthodox marital arrangements as well as within them.

Of cohabitation in Britain, the 1974 Finer Report on One-

Parent Families commented that, 'At no time in history has it been so easy to obtain the sexual and other comforts of marriage without troubling to enter the institution.' Another motive for marriage, namely financial considerations, while doubtless still present, is perhaps of less significance today. The prospective husband's aptitudes, qualifications and professional status are still important as the subsequent family's financial standing is likely to be determined by the husband's economic success or failure, but women are much more likely now to have similar educational and professional qualifications to those of their husbands and if they choose not to marry they can, to a much greater extent than ever before, expect to have a similar career. In the case of men, finding a good housekeeper, mother-substitute, cook and cleaner are doubtless still factors operating in the minds of the more chauvinistic, but the rise in services available and modern household appliances would seem sufficient to enable even the most helpless male to create tolerable conditions in which to endure or enjoy the unmarried state!

So why do people continue to marry, particularly in the light of the much-publicised failure of that fragile institution? American sociologist Ira Reiss answers that the two most powerful groups that are involved in courtship embody the two most basic motivations for people to marry. The powerful groups are parents and young people. The two motives are the parental emphasis on a sense of duty and the desire to maintain one's social standing and the young person's desire for an intense, emotionally satisfying and durable relationship.

In countries such as India and Egypt, where parents still exercise the dominant power, the young are taught to co-operate with their parents in the choice of a mate and to marry from a sense of duty to their family and their community. In countries such as the United States, Britain, Sweden and Hungary, where it is the young who hold the power, the main motives for marriage appear to be the satisfactions arising from a stable, emotionally intimate relationship. In other societies, including Kenya, Japan, Italy and Ireland, young people are asserting their needs to an ever-increasing extent but the opinions of family and community may still exercise substantial influence.

In all instances, sexual satisfaction may well be a motivating factor for marriage but it seems unlikely that it is a significant one. Initial desire for sexual experience supports much of the 'dating' that goes on in society and it may well be the initial attraction in relationships that graduate to love. Sexual interest is obviously pursued but, in general, marital partners are sought for primarily non-sexual reasons bound up with emotional rapport, constancy and support. For example, in a Market and Opinion Research International (MORI) poll of British adults in 1982, 'sexual compatibility' was ranked below 'give and take/equality/understanding' and 'love and affection' in the list of qualities rated as necessary for a happy marriage. Many social surveys conducted in Britain during the 1970s and early 1980s have confirmed such a ranking. In addition, they testify to the remarkable popularity of marriage. In a commercial survey undertaken by McCann Erickson in 1977, only 5 per cent of fifteen- to nineteen-year-olds of both sexes said they would not marry or did not know, while a *Sun* newspaper survey of teenagers' attitudes in 1980 claimed that most teenagers want marriage, parenthood and a happy home life in the future. Sexual fulfilment, while a goal, was not top of the list.

In Hungary, the decision to marry is affected, like everything else there, by considerations of housing. This is the case for one teenage couple interviewed by *Lovelaw*. Zoltan Timar, a nineteen-year-old factory worker, met Ilona Varga, an eighteen-year-old schoolgirl, in a local café. Instantly physically attracted to each other, they slept together within days and decided to marry within weeks. Their plans were to have three to four children (not typically Hungarian, the average being two) and build their own home (very typically Hungarian). Eger, the town in which they live, is a traditionally Catholic, medium-sized town of 75,000 people in the eastern part of the country. It is afflicted by the chronic housing shortage which is a feature of all Hungary. Many young Hungarians devote the first ten years of their married life literally building their own homes with their own hands! Ilona and Zoltan, with some financial assistance from the Hungarian State Bank and their parents, bought their plot on Youth Street in Eger, a street of vacant plots and houses in varying states of completion where a generation of young lovers struggle to put a bricks-and-mortar foundation to their newly established emotional relationships.

Sadly, the foundations of teenage marriage the world over,

and Hungary is no exception, are a good deal weaker than those of the home-made houses. Most of the young couples in Hungary who take on Zoltan and Ilona's burdens end up fairly smartly in the divorce courts. Many of the features of the Ilona-Zoltan romance, and they seemed an engagingly romantic couple very much in love, spell transience – the casual, informal encounter in a café, the brief consolidation of attraction and mutual interest in disco-bars and dance-halls, the rapid sexual consummation and the mutual desire to get out from parental control in their cramped family homes. Not surprisingly, the cold douche of reality represented by financial difficulties, poor job prospects and the actual arrival of the first of those desired four children often proves too much for such frail foundations. Yet Ilona and Zoltan's aspirations are shared by the teenagers of Los Gatos, the schoolchildren at the Alliance High School in Nairobi, the dating agencies, matrimonial advertisements and lonely-hearts columns that are a feature of life in the developing and the developed world.

The growth of dating agencies in Hungary is seen as a response to the problem of the single person in a society which no longer formalises and institutionalises processes enabling young men and young women to get to know each other better without immediately having sex and contemplating marriage. In Hungary, there are three-quarters of a million single, divorced and widowed people over the age of eighteen out of a total of 11 million. In Budapest alone, there are 250,000 single adults, 80 per cent women. This disproportionately high number of women can only partially be attributed to the longer life expectancy of women who lose their spouses earlier than their male counterparts. A particular problem, seen in developing countries such as Egypt as well as in highly industrialised societies such as Japan, is that highly educated women have difficulty finding a marriage partner. In addition, single women and single men are often in the wrong place. In Hungary, for example, a disproportionately large number of single women are to be found in the cities, whereas among males a disproportionately large number are to be found in the villages. Of those men who have not contemplated elementary school, three out of ten appear unable to find a wife. It is a familiar story – too many women in the cities and too highly

A video dating agency in Budapest. Men and women are questioned on video and prospective partners can view the tapes

qualified; too many men in the country and too poorly qualified. Complicating the problem still further is the fact that since Hungary is near the top of the world divorce league, there is a large number of divorced people looking for a new partner.

The latest attempt to solve this problem in Budapest is the Aphrodite Computer Video Dating Agency. People in search of partners and who come to the agency are filmed while answering a number of questions about their own lives and their expectations regarding a future spouse. The resultant video is then placed in the agency's catalogue and browsing applicants of the opposite sex can scrutinise its contents to see if Mr or Miss Right is there. In fact the bureau has a low rate of matching. This seems due to the fact that, according to the psychologist who headed the Four Seasons bureau in Budapest in 1980, applicants have somewhat rigid expectations. Women want husbands who are tall, optimistic, enjoy their work but like their family too. No one wants anyone who is fat, small or has an unskilled job. Men tend to want young and physically attractive women while women prefer men several years older than themselves. Thus, because of what has been termed the 'age expectation factor' people who might well be quite suited to each other are not matched.

A similar situation exists in a number of countries. In the Soviet Union an attempt has been made to provide a national marriage dating agency. One aspect of this service is the placing of advertisements in local newspapers. So popular is this approach that applicants have to wait months or even years before their advertisements can appear. The shortcomings of dating by advertisement are illustrated by the experience of Valentina, a thirty-eight-year-old divorcee who placed an advertisement in her local Omsk newspaper. Some of the men who replied told her bluntly that they were only interested in a one-night stand. Others, apparently, would come to the arranged meeting-place, look her up and down and then walk off.

The material well-being of a prospective partner counts for something in communist countries. In Hungary, those people with apartments have a very much better chance of obtaining a partner than those who do not. In the Soviet Union, a woman who included a four-room flat, a saloon car and a brick garage among her assets was overwhelmed by the replies. In a way, the computerised marriage service is a somewhat modernised version of the old marriage market in which girls were displayed with their dowries and the socially and economically most suitable partners were matched. It would appear that communist standards concerning the classless society have not been able to alter certain popular expectations when it comes to marriage. Like traditional marriage matchmaking, the computerised system emphasises the importance of pairing people with similar educational, financial and social backgrounds.

In China, too, party officials struggle to play Cupid by ordering the setting up of matchmaking agencies to combat what is seen to be a serious social problem, namely the number of single people over thirty. In 1984, the *People's Daily* called for special care for 'elderly bachelors and spinsters' and recommendations were made that healthy social activities such as dancing, concerts, films and talks would be organised to bring the over-thirties together.

In India, matchmaking agencies and matchmakers flourish and there is likewise the custom of placing matrimonial advertisements in virtually every newspaper. However, unlike the paragraphs in lonely-hearts columns, the Indian adver- tisements are placed not by the individuals themselves but by their families. In India, when two people marry the institution brings together two extended families economically as well as socially. Not surprisingly, the family members, and in particu- lar the parents-in-law, actively engage in the search for and approval of any prospective marriage partner. Even college- educated young people accept this, although in general they expect to see and approve their prospective partner and, per- haps, get to know them a little – *after* the engagement. The matrimonial advertisements read not unlike those for second- hand cars, specifying size (that is, height and figure), model (caste), age and even colour (the fairer-skinned the girl the more she will be in demand). The provision by the girl's family of a dowry is no longer legal but is widely practised although amongst the middle classes it more often takes the form of jew- ellery and saris than hard cash. The criteria used in judging a girl's suitability are that she should be attractive with no physi- cal deformities, have good deportment, a sober and pleasing personality and be skilled in household duties – and, of course, be a virgin. The boy should be well educated with good pros- pects and from a well-respected and preferably well-off family. Finally, and most importantly, their horoscopes should match.

N. Subramanian is a technical manager with an oil company in India and has two daughters. His first daughter made a 'good' choice in 1969, marrying a man who now works with the Inter- national Monetary Fund in Washington. This marriage the father arranged pretty quickly for he only needed to consult the horoscopes of three young men for an appropriate match and all three fitted. His second daughter posed more of a problem however. The local astrologer had identified two defects in her horoscope and accordingly N. Subramanian had to find an equivalently defective horoscope to match. Astrological advice was gloomy – quoting chances of 100 to 1 against finding Mr Right. For some three years, while his daughter studied for a BSc in chemistry, he hunted for the elusive match. The search involved scrutiny of 800 horoscopes but eventually he was successful. Asked by *Lovelaw* how a scientifically-minded and educated man like himself could place such faith in astrology,

N. Subramanian replied simply that his own life experience had taught him to trust the horoscope. Born a poor man, he had been told repeatedly by those who interpreted his horoscope that he would do very well in life. He had done, and in a number of remarkable instances predictions based on the horoscope were fulfilled. 'So to that extent,' concluded N. Subramanian, 'I have a lot of belief in astrology but I do not take it as 100 per cent correct. To a remarkable extent astrological predictions are correct but you can only take the horoscope as a yardstick and not the absolute end of the matter.' The marriage has apparently turned out well, the couple are happy and N. Subramanian is the proud grandfather of a one-year-old boy.

Whatever the scientific pretensions of the horoscope, the Indian model of arranged marriage, and it is a model to be found in societies elsewhere in Asia, the Middle East and North Africa, seems attractively pragmatic. For example, the personality and household skills of the girl are understandably rated

S. Gourishankar, a well-known astrologer in Mylapore, Madras. His task is to provide a matrimonial horoscope matching service for the parents of marriageable boys and girls. A bad match, it is believed, can lead to widowhood, incompatibility or childlessness

highly given the fact that after marriage she will be living with her husband's family for many years and her ability and willingness will be under scrutiny. Traditionally, the matchmaking has been done by the older male members of the family who keep an eye on suitable families in the vicinity from the moment the young girl or boy is born. Talk of marriage starts when the children are still young, partly because marriage is such a crucial institution (the 'wrong' choice can shame an entire family and wreck the marriage prospects of the other children) and partly because people, particularly women, marry very young in India. With increased mobility, however, it has become difficult in towns to find suitable families for marriage so advertisements and matchmaking have become even more popular. The matchmaker, who may be the local barber, is often approached by parents with marriageable children. The use of such a middleman enables face to be saved should either of the parties pull out of negotiations.

Other assistance in the process is sought through prayer. Outside the magnificent Kamakshi Temple near Madras can be seen queues of women and their daughters. The story goes that the goddess Kamakshi, by doing a severe penance, found a husband. As a result, if any unmarried girl comes and offers a vow to the goddess she too will obtain her life match. Another novel approach involves social evenings organised by caste groups, which help their members find jobs, accommodation and a matrimonial contact. In Madras, one of the organisations, known as the Triple S, runs regular evening meetings at which fathers of children of marriageable age stand up and give an account of themselves, their family and the kind of match they are seeking. In some instances, the hopeful boy or, less frequently, girl may attend and address the meeting.

What of arranged marriage as a method of arriving at the right choice? One person well positioned to answer is Sikh writer Sharan-Jeet Shan whose book In My Own Name[1] was published in Britain in 1985. She makes it plain that when a marriage is arranged with the complete consent of both partners and a thorough appraisal of each other's background it stands a very good chance of success, maybe even a better chance than so-called 'love marriages'. The crucial qualification is 'complete consent'. Many young Indians look somewhat askance at

A matrimonial evening in Madras organised by the Triple S Society. The young woman describes the kind of qualities that she would like her prospective husband to possess

Western customs and the emphasis on individual choice with its seemingly chaotic consequences of separation, divorce and one-parent families. The arranged marriage has the advantage that crucial and explicit aspects of the marriage contract – the emphasis on permanence, on fidelity and on constancy – are underpinned and interlocked with pragmatic and measurable qualities such as income, religious persuasion, educational status and household skills.

The disadvantages of the arranged marriage become very apparent when consent is impaired or even absent and/or when the arranged marriage system is transplanted to a very different culture. Sharan-Jeet Shan's story makes the point tellingly. A nineteen-year-old studying medicine in the Punjab, she fell in love with and secretly married a Muslim student. Her father discovered the truth, refused to recognise the marriage, locked her in her aunt's house and beat her. After eight months her resistance broke and she agreed to marry a man chosen for her by her father although she was warned not to expect too much from it for she was 'spoilt goods'. This arranged husband turned out to be a thirty-year-old uneducated stranger living in England. She joined him in 1966, giving up her medical career, and was consigned to a life in which she was adjured by her mother-in-law never to call her husband by his first name, never to question his judgements, always to show him respect and obedience and always to veil when in mixed company. Eventually she left her husband, made a new life with her two children and published her story on behalf of the many Asian women in Britain bound within loveless marriages and in the hope that their parents might begin to question their traditional attitudes towards daughters. In an interview in *The Times* in October 1985, she declared,

> Few people outside the Asian community can comprehend the awfulness of life in Britain for bewildered Asian women who arrive here from small Indian villages and try to settle in urban ghetto areas. It is difficult for outsiders to understand the attitudes of a culture where 'bridal pyres' are still lit to get rid of women who have no dowry or husband. Although it is widely held that this cruel custom no longer exists, every year in India several hundred young women, some the mothers of very young children, are beaten to death or burned alive during an 'accidental' fire simply because they are considered a burden on their families.

Another society in which arranged marriages are practised and where the subject is controversial is Egypt. At the present time the country is in the grip of an ideological ferment, pulled towards both Western values and standards and Islamic fundamentalism. On the streets of Cairo this conflict finds representation amongst Egyptian women in that some are veiled and some are not. The majority of women in the Parliament's People's Assembly are veiled as are a sizeable proportion of young women at Cairo University. The wearing of the veil is variously interpreted. In the words of one Egyptian female commentator, Fatna Sabbah, 'The veil has a very precise meaning: it represents the denial of the economic dimension of women who, according to the tenets of Muslim orthodoxy, are exclusively sexual beings.' In contrast, the Egyptian film *The Veiled Revolution*, made by Elizabeth Fernea, insists that in taking on the veil Egyptian women are embracing authentic Arab culture and are thus moving forward on their own terms rather than on those of Western capitalism. Nawal el Saadawi, the author of an influential and controversial Egyptian book entitled *The Hidden Face of Eve*,[2] disagrees and argues that as Egyptian unemployment began to rise recently so the veil began to be resurrected. One of its essential purposes is to remove women from the job market and consolidate and confirm them in a sexist role which maintains male domination and power. The complexity of this is illustrated by the comment of a university student quoted in *Women: A World Report*[3] to the effect that the veiled woman covers herself and thereby declares herself to be of good moral standing, whereas the girl who for whatever reason prefers to remain unveiled may well signal to Egyptian men that she is morally loose, sexually available and probably promiscuous.

Once again we are confronted with the fact that once a society starts to change and more choices become available, rigid customs which have hitherto provided a structure for society start to cause problems. The case history of Amina Sobhy illustrates the point. A thirty-year-old single woman living in Cairo, she is a firm Muslim and respecter of a belief system

An Egyptian contract-signing ceremony. The bride sits in a separate room while her father signs the marriage contract on her behalf

which insists that she has no right to become acquainted with a young man, meet with him, go out with him, even sit alone with him outside her house. So how does she make the right choice of partner, indeed any choice in sprawling, fragmented Cairo, a city of 11 million people? She is an educated woman, a qualified architect, an avid reader and lover of literature, particularly poetry. She readily accepts the religious restrictions upon her movements and insists that had she a daughter she would not want her to behave in any other way.

Amina's brother, who runs the family shoe-making business, reveals that a husband has been found for his sister through the good offices of a matchmaker. The prospective husband, Salah Eldesouky, is brought to the house where he meets Amina in the presence of the other members of her family. Then Salah brings his brothers and sisters to the house and together they all read a religious text as a sign of a formal link. Only after this can he meet Amina on formal occasions when another member of her family is present. Conversation centres on highly practical matters – Salah's religious convictions (strongly fundamentalist, like Amina's), his education (to a lower level than Amina), work (he runs his own video maintenance store and develops film for the Egyptian Academy of Art) and his character (hardworking). Having turned down other men on previous occasions, Amina this time agrees, leaving Lovelaw wondering how much the fact that her mother seemed to think that being unmarried at thirty meant a lifetime on the shelf had had something to do with it. When asked the place of love in all of this, Amina simply replies that love comes after she learns to understand him during the engagement period, through becoming used to each other and being familiar with each other. Salah, for his part, takes an equally pragmatic, unromantic view. When one chooses a wife the first thing to consider is her background, her father, mother, sisters, brothers. 'They are all like a mirror that reflects her behaviour,' he declares and from the reflection he is quite prepared to make up his mind about the sort of person she is. He does not think too highly of the Western way of arranging marriages – his brother in America has just married on the basis of romantic love. Salah himself is anxious to marry. He feels he knows Amina and besides he has a flat which needs looking after, he works long hours and needs a helping spouse urgently. The recent death of his mother has left him without anyone to tend to his domestic needs. He does not have the time or indeed the inclination to fall in love. Love, and here he echoes his intended spouse, will come in time.

In Japan, marriage has long been characterised by the tradition of *o-miai* by which a go-between who knows both families introduces the man and woman concerned. The couple then meet socially over a period of time and decide whether they wish to marry or not. In practice, this can be a relatively informal process whereby friends introduce the girl and boy to each other. *O-miai* is a structured approach to the problem of providing people whose social circles may be rather limited with the opportunity to meet eligible people of the opposite sex. Quite frequently the company boss will act as *o-miai* to two

In Japan brides often have three changes of clothes during the wedding ceremony: a kimono, as in this picture, a white Western wedding dress and a white traditional wedding kimono

employees, and after their marriage act as a consultant in times of trouble or need. According to surveys carried out by the Japanese Ministry of Health and Welfare, marriages through o-miai, which stood at 49·8 per cent of all marriages in 1966, were down to 36·2 per cent in 1973, reflecting the increasing trend of finding one's partner on one's own.

Advocates of the arranged method of choice emphasise that, far from such marriages being 'blind', each party knows a great deal about the other before the contract is ever signed. Or at least those things that matter are known. There is the rub. In those societies where the woman's ability to undertake the household duties and the man's ability to work hard and conscientiously and bring home the goods are the primary requirements, then the premarital assessment can be carried out thoroughly and, indeed, relatively effectively without the two parties immediately concerned playing much of a role. Their emotional needs are valued low on the list and the assumption is that if they undertake their primary duties adequately love is as likely to follow as not.

Contrasted with the often elaborate methods of arranging a marriage in societies such as India and Egypt, the Western approach seems positively cavalier. Young people in the West appear influenced by the vague desire to forge an emotional bond with someone who, with luck, will strengthen their self-confidence with positive declarations of love and support and who, in turn, will be the object of equivalently intense emotions. The satisfaction of such desires is much less easy to bring about and indeed to measure than when the purpose of marriage is to have a partner who will help organise day-to-day living. Even Western individuals used to self-analysis are often quite unable to determine their emotional needs and priorities. The Hungarian sociologist Laszlo Czeh-Szombathy writes in the *New Hungarian Quarterly* that the circumstances in which prospective marital partners meet in the West are favourable to the playing of roles (he could be talking of Ilona and Zoltan and their regular meetings in the disco-bars of Eger). Such role-playing 'prevents the manifestation of their essential qualities. Conflicts are avoided which display one's character to the full. They marry without sufficient information about the things which are the most important for marriage today.'

Above Young men and
women mix freely in
Japan but when it
comes to marriage
often parents make
the final decision

Right Two young punk
lovers from Britain

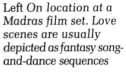

Left On location at a
Madras film set. Love
scenes are usually
depicted as fantasy song-
and-dance sequences

Far left above The
second step towards
the arranged marriage
of this young couple
is the girl-seeing
ceremony. The pair
already know quite a
lot about each other
from their parents but
this is the first time
they have actually
seen each other. If this
meeting is successful
they will be married a
few weeks later

Below The fantasy of
romantic love features
prominently on the
giant film-hoardings in
Madras

Above The wedding of a couple in south India is announced not only to the family but to the community as the procession progresses from the bride's home to the temple

Below Immediately after the wedding ceremony, the wife serves her husband a meal. In return he ties a bundle of money to her sari. These acts symbolise their future roles

Hungary has devised its own secular ceremony to replace the traditional Christian church service. This is performed in the local town hall (above) but old traditions die hard and even after the secular ceremony the wedding party will proceed across town to be blessed in a church (below)

Above left A Sunday outing for all the family is a rare treat in Japan where the father tends to spend much of his spare time with his work colleagues. Here Mr Fujisawa enjoys a picnic in the country

Below left Young girls being prepared for marriage at Ikenobo College, Kyoto. Flower arranging, performing tea ceremonies and administrating the household are all regarded as necessary skills for the good Japanese wife

Above right The influence of American culture – television programmes, fast food and fashion – on Japanese teenagers is widespread. This is a fifties' fashion parade in Tokyo's Harajuku Park

Below right In an overcrowded city like Tokyo there is little privacy for young couples. The Japanese solution is the love hotel where rooms can be hired by the hour. Each room has a different theme and is fully equipped with porn videos and condom dispensers. There are over 35,000 of these hotels in Japan

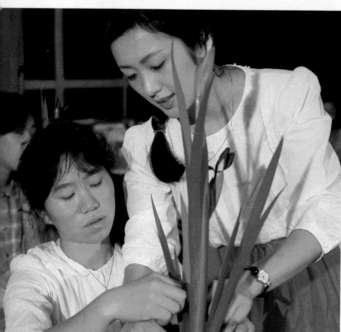

Above *An Italian bride in her wedding dress. Young Italian brides consider their appearance to be of paramount importance and will spend months planning what to wear for their wedding*

Left *A man looking after a baby and performing domestic chores may be a typical scene in Sweden but research shows that elsewhere men still leave the housework to their wives*

Emotional demands change more easily than economic ones, although economic development can of course give rise to conflicts if one of the partners, as a result say of promotion or a rapid increase in earnings, alters his or her priorities. Emotional needs, however, are bound to change and especially so if one or both of the partners are young at the time of the marriage. The way partners communicate, their sexual intimacies, their experiences – all change. The balance of emotional demands remains the same only if both strive more or less consciously and continuously to develop together during marriage.

Another problem with Western marriage, say the critics, is that often all that is left to signify that it is a solemn and binding institution is the actual wedding ceremony itself. As entry into and exit from marriage becomes more casual and its legal status weakens, the wedding becomes ever more elaborate as if to ensure that by a really big and flamboyant show on the day the vow of loyalty, permanence and mutual trust can be underwritten.

In Italy, the cynics claim that apart from the irresistible power of love young people get married because of the wedding ceremony itself and the pressures of home-based consumerism. 'How many romantic dreams,' asks journalist Natalia Aspesi waspishly in the Rome newspaper *La Repubblica*,

> revolve around the iron with the adjustable steam jet, the set of white saucepans decorated with red hearts which match the napkins, the dusters and the sheets, and the silver bottle-holder with an insulated lining? How many lonely evenings are spent between kisses, dreaming over the horrible appliance for making fondues, the useless trout smoker, the silver mats for twelve people, the coffee service for twenty-four?

Another Italian journalist, Luisa Espanet, who replies to readers' letters in *Vogue Sposa*, says that the great majority of the letters are from future brides asking for help and advice on the ceremony and the wedding dress. 'It is especially young women under twenty-five who write to us,' she says, 'and above all from the South and the small towns. The only thing that interests them is really their appearance which they study down to the tiniest detail for months and months, from hairstyle to dress, jewellery, tights and shoes.' She adds that she is sometimes tempted to agree that many a young woman's reason for getting married is the personal splendour of the wedding day.

Not that things are very different in Britain. 'Girls buy *Brides* when they're getting married the same way as people buy *Parker's Price Guide* when they're looking for a second-hand car,' the editor of *Brides* magazine recently declared in a newspaper interview. The magazine, launched in 1955, provides a detailed catalogue of social gaffes to be avoided at weddings, a cornucopia of wedding-list consumer durables, a parade of bridal fashions and ecstatic recollections of last year's brides. The magazine caters to a highly specific and lucrative market. The 160,000 couples who every year have a white wedding in Britain (70 per cent of all first marriages) embark on the biggest spending binge of their lives. On average, they will spend £3500 on the wedding and £1000 on the honeymoon, not to mention substantial expenditure on household goods. Sixtynine per cent put down their first mortgage payment on a house or flat.

Such lavishness need not however spell superficiality. In the small southern Italian town of Catanzaro the right choice is made in a way which is similar to the way choices are made in Britain. One difference is that young people in Italy are far more dependent on their families and very rarely move away from the family home until they marry. Even after marriage, they are more likely to see considerably more of their parents than does the average British couple. So it is hardly surprising that while a young Italian couple will probably choose each other freely, their choice is likely to be discussed and influenced by other family members, most notably parents. Unlike the situation in India, boys and girls mix freely, but sex before marriage, and certainly before the engagement, is strongly disapproved of, while cohabitation, even in the more liberal North, is positively eccentric. When it comes to making the right choice, love and security are the familiar key factors. For the boy (and his family) the sexual reputation of the girl is important. For the girl (and her family) the boy should be well established in his career. The average age of marriage is around twenty-five for both sexes. A dowry and trousseau (*il corredo*) are still expected but there is a highly practical flavour to them – not the jewellery and saris of Indian dowries, more likely a colour television set. In a town the size of Catanzaro (with a population of 100,000) the families of the young couple are likely at least to know of each other and can easily find out important details and the existence of any cupboard skeletons.

Over 80 per cent of weddings in Catanzaro take place in church and every couple getting married has to attend preparation classes with the local priest. Many young couples do so reluctantly because they feel that the Church places too much emphasis on marriage as a sacrament and not enough on practical problems such as contraception. However, there is much evidence that the Church is trying to respond to these very problems; in Catanzaro, for example, young priests try to organise social activities for young people so that they can feel the Church is indeed concerned with their welfare.

In truth, it is far from easy to know how to respond to the issues that are raised by the shift in the factors influencing the choice of spouse, to know quite how to prepare people for marriage in the modern world. The more basic, prosaic even, expectations of traditional marriage no longer apply or have lost much of their force. In today's society, with its widespread contraception, cohabitation and abortion, there is no longer any reason to marry for sexual enjoyment or for the joys of living with one's beloved. More liberal attitudes towards illegitimacy have made forced marriages a phenomenon of the past. Women have less and less need to marry for financial or social advancement, although many men may still seek a mate to keep the home fires burning while they carve their paths of progress in the great world outside. Only two real motives remain and both pose problems. The first is the search through marriage for happiness. Contemporary marriage more and more resembles a vehicle for self-exploration and self-discovery in which the partner is a co-therapist and the end result, whether it be mutual fulfilment or separation, is regarded by both participants as 'personal growth'. The problem is that for many marriage cannot live up to such a high demand.

But couples still marry to have children. Indeed, the only purpose of marriage as a social institution warranting public interest and involvement in what is otherwise a private and intimate relationship is the parenting of children. The problem is that society is often thoroughly confused as it applies the values and attitudes which belong more understandably with one notion of marriage, namely the values of fidelity and sacrifice, to a quite different and in some instances a quite contrary notion, namely marriage as a facilitator of self-development. That the choice be right is important for the two participants in their search for themselves through the other. It becomes imperative when one of the outcomes of that choice is the creation of a new human life. It is then that the expectations placed on modern marriage look so frail and inappropriate and the more practical values of traditional marriage look just that little bit less anachronistic. But the changing roles of wives and husbands within marriage mean that making the right choice in any society is becoming increasingly like a shot in the dark.

3 WIVES AND HUSBANDS

The patient who sat in my outpatient clinic was a forty-two-year-old married nurse complaining of fatigue. She had already been to her general practitioner who, having ruled out anaemia, sent her to a hormone specialist. No, there was nothing wrong with her thyroid but she did seem depressed and she did weep a tear or two in the presence of the sympathetic endocrinologist, so he wondered whether she might be seriously depressed and suggested she see me. Fatigue is indeed a common symptom of depressive illness but Mrs A did not look depressed so much as exhausted. Indeed, she was the first patient I had seen that day who seemed more tired than me! When she told me the details of her typical day I began to feel exhausted too.

For Mrs A is one of today's emancipated women. She is a full-time career woman *and* she is a wife and mother. She is a member of what sociologists call a 'dual earner couple'. Her husband is also a busy man, working as a line manager with a major car manufacturing company. However, when he accompanied his wife on a follow-up visit I noticed that he did not look the slightest bit tired or depressed. Asked for his view as to why his wife felt so washed out, he replied without hesitation, 'She does too much.'

The 'too much' that Mrs A had been doing was the job of superwoman that more and more women are called upon to do. She was a very active, conscientious and efficient ward sister on a demanding intensive care unit in one of London's teaching hospitals and she undertook the cleaning, cooking and laundry for herself, her husband and her two sons, aged twelve and eight. Indeed, so typical was Mrs A's experience that she was quite reluctant to accept that such a demanding dual role might be at least a contributory cause of her emotional strain. 'But,' she protested, 'lots of women have a day like mine and they don't all end up seeing a psychiatrist.' That I and my colleagues don't see more may, of course, be a reflection of the stoical resilience of women in general rather than of any emotional fragility of Mrs A in particular.

The changing role of women in modern society is a product not merely of greater access to employment but of an increasing access to education, a growing degree of control over childbearing and changes in the relationship between spouses. But it is the developments in employment that at first glance seem most remarkable. In Britain fifty years ago, less than 10 per cent of married women were in paid employment. Today, over 50 per cent of married women are in paid employment and married women workers outnumber unmarried women workers by two to one. Overall, 25 per cent of the entire work-force are married women and about half of these care for at least one dependent child.

It is the age of her youngest child, and particularly the presence of a child under five, which is the main determinant of whether or not a woman works outside the home and whether she works full- or part-time. In 1979, only about one in four women whose youngest child was under five was working and of these 75 per cent worked part-time. Despite a widespread assumption to the contrary, it is still very rare for mothers with pre-school children to work full-time. Indeed, only 6 per cent do! But the speed with which a mother returns to some form of employment outside the home after the birth of her child is increasing. Whereas in 1971 only 9 per cent of mothers with new babies were economically active to any extent within a year of the birth, the 1979 national survey of mothers of new babies showed that nearly 25 per cent were economically active by the time their babies were eight months old.

Many mothers have to work out of financial necessity. In 1975 the Central Policy Review Staff, a British government advisory body, estimated that four times as many families would have been in poverty had it not been for wives' earnings. While British society sometimes seems ambivalent about married women working, particularly mothers of young children, social planning and policy have left most such women with little choice. Having gone out to work, whether for financial reasons or for personal fulfilment or both, working mothers are consciously or subconsciously reproached for neglecting either their family and/or their jobs. Having stayed at home to fulfil the role of full-time housewife and mother, women find themselves discredited socially in a society where status is increasingly defined by means of one's own personal economic activity.

But if I claim there is this role conflict for women, why not for men? The answer, of course, lies in the fact that until recently men and women had clearly circumscribed and distinct social roles within marriage. Women worked full-time within the home, looking after the children and caring for their husbands, while men worked outside the home and brought home the money. Such a situation still exists in large parts of the world to this day. However, the increasing employment of women outside the home, whether it be a cause or a consequence of female emancipation, has altered the woman's role. To date, however, there has not been a noticeable change in the male role. Men still do next to nothing in the home!

The average British male in full-time employment works forty-five hours a week compared with just under forty-one hours a week for his full-time female colleague. But when the amount of time the full-time working woman devotes to such tasks as cooking, shopping, child care and washing is added to the equation, she ends up with three hours *less* free time every weekday than her male counterpart. In Italy, 85 per cent of mothers with children and full-time jobs outside the home are married to men who undertake no domestic duties whatsoever. Between 1975 and 1980, several thousand Dutch men and women kept a record for a week of what they had been doing every quarter of an hour. The results showed that Dutch men were doing more housework in 1980 but there were still marked differences between the men and the women: in 1980, women spent an average of twenty-seven hours a week on house duties and the family, men about six and a half hours. In 1975 men devoted twenty-five hours a week to paid employment, women five hours, five years later the comparable figures were twenty-two hours and six hours. It has been estimated that if matters continue to change at this pace, men and women in the Netherlands will eventually spend an equal amount of time on housework and the family in the year 2018!

In Europe as a whole, a working woman has on average only two-thirds of the free time her husband has. Rubbing in the salt,

> According to estimates and projections of the International
> Labour Office, women constitute 35 per cent of the world's labour
> force, and this figure is likely to increase steadily to the year 2000.
> Unless profound and extensive changes are made, the type of
> work available to the majority of women, as well as the rewards,
> will continue to be low. Women's employment is likely to be
> concentrated in areas requiring lower skills and lower wages and
> minimum job security. While women's total input of labour in the
> formal and informal sector will surpass that of men by the year
> 2000, they will receive an unequal share of the world's assets and
> income. According to recent estimates, it seems that women have
> sole responsibility for the economic support of a large number of
> the world's children, approximately one-third and higher in
> some countries, and the numbers seem to be rising.
> Forward-looking strategies must be progressive, equitable and
> designed to support effectively women's roles and
> responsibilities as they evolve up to the year 2000. It will
> continue to be necessary to take specific measures to prevent
> discrimination and exploitation of their economic contribution
> at national and international levels.[1]
>
> United Nations Report, Nairobi, 1985

her domestic duties are not only additional but also unpaid. It
has been estimated that if a household in Holland had to have
all its work done professionally on a paid basis it would cost an
average of 26,500 guilders (£7000) per annum at 1984 prices.
An equivalent assessment in the US suggests that it would cost
$14,500 (£9500) per annum to purchase the services provided
by the average American housewife. On the basis of such
assessments, it is estimated that unpaid housework undertaken
in the industrialised world contributes to between 25 and 40
per cent of gross national product.

The situation with regard to housework is little different in
countries with a centrally organised economic system. In the
Soviet Union more than 92 per cent of able-bodied women,
including those with small children, work outside the home.
They account for 50 per cent of the national labour force. Yet
there has been little change in the amount of work in the domestic setting undertaken by men and women. An average Soviet
working mother is expected to put in eight hours' work, then
rush home and spend a further four to six hours cooking,
washing and cleaning. Her husband sits in front of the tele-

vision or goes out drinking with his mates. Surveys reveal that the Soviet husband of the 1980s does even less in the home than his predecessor did sixty years ago, and in 1984 it was calculated that while men work about fifty hours a week women average eighty hours!

The chief injustice, however, is not so much the extra work that women must do outside the home as the assumption that it is their role and only their role to do all the work within it. And whether they only do housework, only work outside the home or struggle to be 'superwomen' and do both, contemporary women in the developed world are often left with the uneasy feeling that they end up unfulfilled in one way or another. So many women do try to fulfil both aspects of being a woman. However, because of their responsibilities at home, most women are not able to put in the same number of hours as men. Such differences in work paid and unpaid mean that women earn very much less than men. A recent study of twenty-four countries found that in 1975 a woman working in manufacturing industries earned an average of only 70 cents for every dollar earned by a man doing the same work. In 1982, she earned 78 cents. Great regional differences exist. Women in Japan and the Republic of Korea take home less than half the wages earned by men whereas women in Denmark, Sweden, Norway, El Salvador and Burma earn about 20 per cent less than men. Equal-pay legislation does not appear to make a great deal of difference; minimum-pay legislation might be a better approach. In Portugal, the earnings gap nearly halved, with women's wages rising from 52 per cent of men's in 1973 to 71 per cent in 1980, following the introduction of minimum-pay laws.

Differences in paid and unpaid work; differences in hours worked outside and inside the home; differences in promotion prospects and pension arrangements – these are the differences between men and women competing in the market-place outside the home. What effect, if any, have such differences and the trends on which they are based had on the roles of men and women within marriage? In those societies which historically have maintained strictly defined and separate roles for men and women, has the impetus behind women going to work altered these roles?

Lovelaw went to Japan, a society in considerable flux and yet one where appearances suggest the persistence of distinct sex roles and different expectations on the part of men and women concerning marriage. *Lovelaw* filmed a classroom of young Japanese women being prepared for marriage at Ikenobo College in Kyoto. To be a good wife was clearly equated with possessing highly developed skills as a flower arranger, an organiser of the tea ceremony and administrator of the household.

Child-rearing responsibilities are seen to be entirely the Japanese mother's responsibility. So central is motherhood to family life that, after a child is born, the couple quickly begin calling each other 'Mummy' and 'Daddy'. The home is kept separate from work; Japanese wives rarely entertain their husbands' business colleagues.

The Japanese male role is evaluated primarily in terms of his dedication to work and his ability to provide financially for his family. Indeed, Japanese wives expect their husbands to have hungry appetites for work. So important is this that a husband's failure to succeed figures prominently in marital quarrels. In a 1976 survey conducted by the Japanese newspaper *Sankei Ribingu*, entitled 'A Collection of Tabooed Words that Depress Husbands', insults such as 'Your pay is low', 'You haven't got the guts to succeed' and demeaning comparisons with other husbands' salaries ranked high on the list.

The extent of this classic separation of roles in contemporary Japan is analysed by writer and commentator on women's issues, Keiko Higuchi. She recently observed that there is no lack of difficulties between Japanese wives and husbands, especially where salaried workers are concerned, 'since their respective daily lives have absolutely nothing in common'. Nor does Higuchi expect things to change,

> While bearing in mind the conditions of contemporary family life, it may be interesting to imagine the situation thirty years from now. If the husband is a typical contemporary male, he will be a company employee who has experienced several moves, including transfers leaving his family behind. In spite of these disruptions, he will still be able to feel some continuity of his life through his work. His wife, though, will by no means experience a comparable sense of continuity, since with every move she must rebuild the uprooted home and family life from scratch. Husband and wife will spend most of their time performing their respective roles with-

out interfering in each other's affairs, the husband at work and his wife taking care of the household. The only thing they will have in common will be their children.[2]

Mr and Mrs Fujisawa bear out such predictions today. Mrs Michiyo Fujisawa was a schoolteacher for three years before marrying her husband when she was twenty-three and he a twenty-six-year-old textile manager. She stopped working full-time after the birth of her first child and now teaches maths part-time in their Kyoto home, while also looking after her two children, aged twelve and eight, and her husband. She sees her role in terms of giving Mr Shigetaka Fujisawa 'rest and comfort, both physically and mentally, when he comes home tired from work' and 'to do as much as possible to make the home conducive to that.' But Mr Fujisawa, like the average Japanese salaried executive, does not spend a great deal of time in his home. Every weekday he leaves for work around 7 am and he does not get home until after midnight. Saturday is spent playing golf with business colleagues. Sunday is his day not merely of rest but of making contact with his wife and children.

What is Mr Fujisawa doing until midnight? After work, he goes drinking with his colleagues to his favourite hostess-bar in downtown Osaka. It is, he tells us, an activity which Japanese men regard as customary and manly. His wife's only complaint is that he does not always tell her if he is not coming back at night. At the hostess-bar, Mr Fujisawa cuddles the hostesses, sings to taped background music and ruminates on the fact that within the confines of Japanese marriage neither partner expects the Western notion of love.

What Mrs Fujisawa cannot expect is to have the same freedom of movement outside the home as her husband. If she is not present when her husband returns from work, he may respond with irritation or downright hostility. His response reflects his need for domestic services – indeed, it is said that a Japanese husband on returning home says three words – bath, food and bed. Of course a Japanese husband's irritation over not receiving his dinner on time does not distinguish him from many a British or American counterpart; indeed, Mr A, whose wife attended me for 'dual earner couple' fatigue, admitted that he found it difficult to restrain himself from comment when confronted with unmade beds on return from work – but the intensity of the restriction of wives' outings is far greater in Japan. According to Samuel Coleman, author of *Family Planning in Japanese Society*,[3] if and how often the wife is out after 6 pm is a matter of negotiation with the husband. Wives who are seen alone in public in the late evening, when it is assumed that their husbands are returning home, can be the subject of gossip. Coleman adds that even data on hours of sleep portray a disadvantageous domestic interaction for Japanese women. 'In a near-reversal of the European pattern,' he writes, 'Japanese wives have less time for sleep than their husbands.' According to one international survey, Japanese wives had almost one hour less sleeping time per day than the average for European housewives. The difference results from the wife's duties and obligations, among them rising early to prepare the family breakfast and staying up at night to greet her husband returning from his late-night business entertaining.

Yet the employment trends which in Britain indicate that change is underway are perceptible in contemporary Japan too. By 1978, Japanese women constituted one-third of the national work-force. More than half of all employed women are over thirty-five and nearly two-thirds are married. The increase in the percentage of married women holding jobs is, of course, indicative of the marked rise in the number of middle-aged women entering the work-force after their children have grown up but there is a tendency on the part of younger women to enter long-term employment. This increase in the number of women playing non-domestic roles is leading to demands for changes in the life-style of the family but Japan has been slow to adapt to these needs. 'To achieve success as a professional,' writes Masako Amano, associate professor of sociology at Kinjo Gakuin University, 'a man must first of all sacrifice his role as a family man.' In contrast, women have always been expected to give priority to their domestic tasks and it is still not acceptable for a woman to sacrifice these roles for the sake of career success. Housework, child care, and especially the care of the sick and the elderly are for the most part regarded as women's work. As for men modifying their roles within the family, there are but slight signs of any change.

Rising educational standards, according to North American and European experience, should bring a proportionate increase in the percentage of so-called nuclear families and changes in sex roles as more and more women venture outside the home to pursue careers. Some changes of attitude regarding the concept of role differentiation on the basis of sex are indeed detectable. Opinion polls conducted by the Japanese Prime Minister's Office have shown that the proportion of people who approve of the notion that men belong in the workplace and women in the home has dramatically declined from 83 per cent in 1972 to 30 per cent in 1979.

Yet with increasing educational opportunities for women, sex-role stereotypes remain surprisingly influential. At Japanese universities the largest numbers of female students enrol for literary courses followed by those in education. Fewer women are found in engineering, science and agriculture. Teaching, nursing, pharmacy and dietetics remain traditional occupations for women whereas medicine and law remain male bastions. Professor Amano distinguishes between what she terms the 'semi-professions' such as nursing and teaching and the established professions, medicine, law, architecture, engineering, dominated by men. Between these two groups, around the world, remain wide differences in income and social status. Such sex-role stereotypes intriguingly mirror the supposed differences in aptitude and interest between the sexes. Thus, for example, occupations such as secretaries, filing clerks, cleaners and canteen workers neatly dovetail with women's traditional roles of supporting and cleaning up after men – it is hardly surprising that they are seen as 'women's jobs' and remain relatively poorly paid in many countries.

More intriguing and depressing still is the suggestion that as women penetrate a profession so its status falls. In the Soviet Union women have eroded male dominance in medicine so that today 80 per cent of doctors there are women. However, as this percentage rose over the years so the status of medicine fell, so that today the average non-specialised doctor earns less than a skilled industrial worker. But specialist doctors, senior medical academics and medical administrators, the over-whelming majority of whom are male, have maintained their income and status superiority.

Commenting on the fall in status of general medicine in the Soviet Union while specialist medicine and academic medicine maintain their high ranking, sociologist Ira Reiss argues that the medical establishment 'instead of yielding to egalitarian pressures merely accommodated women into a new version of a male-dominated profession. This occurrence,' he concludes, 'supports the view that a new system of gender equality first necessitates equality of power and prestige in the overall culture.' However, as Reiss is the first to admit, this is a catch-22 situation in that before the overall culture will assign such equality to men and women the individual institutions have to incorporate the equality. Furthermore, there is the difficulty that for such changes to occur there must be a shift in thinking, not just among the women but amongst the very men that are in power.

Not surprisingly, those women who succeed in such male-dominated bastions as law, medicine and politics are, statistically at any rate, exceptions when compared with women at large. In contrast, male politicians are statistically more representative of their male non-leader contemporaries. Women politicians sacrifice more for their position, they are less often married, have fewer children and are better trained than other women. Commenting on the European situation, a British political researcher, Joni Lovenduski, points out that, whereas marriage appears a positive resource for male politicians, being unattached increases a woman's chances of success in terms of career and public life. When women do penetrate the higher levels of political power, we see the old familiar signs of sex-role stereotyping at work once more!

> Women leaders tend still to be assigned to posts in the 'soft' ministries of family, welfare, culture and, except where this is considered to be an important post, education. Such posts tend not to lead to further promotion in that they do not provide the experience of high-level management of economic or foreign affairs considered to be important in top leadership selection. On the other hand, they provide important channels of promotion for women.[4]

Meanwhile, Mrs Fujisawa, like many Japanese women and indeed women the world over, puts most of her emotional energy into rearing her children. She kept the umbilical cords of both her children and showed them proudly to a somewhat nonplussed *Lovelaw* cameraman. She wishes her husband would come home a little earlier and share her worries concerning the task, which largely devolves to her, of negotiating the children through the formidable and demanding hurdles of the Japanese examination system. She wishes too that there was more sharing and less separation. She admits that while she does tend to take the day-to-day household decisions in her case it is her husband who controls the family budget. (It is very common for the wife to control the family finances – even for the husband to hand over his salary each month to his wife while he receives in return an allowance.) However, they do indeed discuss financial matters when eventually Mr Fujisawa comes home at night but since he is every so often a little exhausted by the demands of his bar socialising, not every discussion is particularly fruitful.

Much of the Japanese experience is readily comprehensible to any British observer. In parts of the developing world, however, sex-role differentiation takes much more dramatic forms and the traditional separation of the sex roles acquires all the appearance of formidable discrimination. In parts of South East Asia, female mortality begins to exceed male mortality shortly after birth, a reversal of the trend seen virtually everywhere else in the world. During the critical period from the first to the eleventh month of life the female death rate was 21 per cent higher than that of males, according to one survey undertaken by the Government of Bangladesh. Other studies in this part of the world show that infant girls receive much less care and attention than boys even if female infanticide by means of drowning in vessels of milk or the administration of opium is no longer practised. While protein-calorie malnutrition has been found to be four or five times more common among girls, boys outnumber girls by fifty to one in hospitalised patient samples. While comparable numbers of boys and girls suffer from diarrhoea, boys exceed girls in treatment facilities by 66 per cent.

According to Shushum Bhatia, a scientist with the International Centre for Diarrhoeal Disease Research in Bangladesh, not only do parents underinvest in the care, feeding and health care of female children but 'they also have a tendency to invest more heavily in their sons' than their daughters' education'. Such discrimination is reflected in the comparatively low literacy rates for women and it is particularly discouraging because studies of child mortality have shown that it is twice as high for children of mothers with no education than for those with elementary education. The difference becomes four times higher for mothers with no education than those with secondary education.

Traditional practices regarding marriage and the status of daughters-in-law in the household, along with practices associated with pregnancy, childbirth, lactation, fertility control and health care utilisation, further aggravate the health impairment of women. Among rural societies of the Indian subcontinent, parents wish to marry off their daughters as soon as they attain puberty. This custom precludes girls from achieving an educational status comparable to that of boys – in those social classes where boys do go to schools – and this lack of education then prevents women from seeking alternative roles in life. Despite the ban on child marriage in most countries, marriages in the early teens are widely prevalent. In certain areas of Bangladesh, girls may get married while thirteen to fourteen years old and could be back in the parents' home by the age of fifteen to sixteen – divorced.[5]

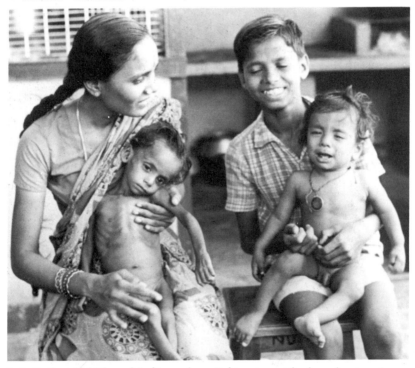

In both Bangladesh and India preferential treatment for boys begins at birth and is reflected in the mortality statistics of girls and women. These babies are two-year-old twins: a girl on the left and a boy on the right

In many African countries too the birth of a girl has often been regarded as a misfortune and the rites that mark the stages of life emphasise the differences between the sexes. Boubacar Diallo, working with the Ministry of Public Health in Mali, points out that now, as in the past, the main victim of many of the traditional customs that have been grafted on the Islamic social organisations remains the woman,

> Accused of fickleness, instability, physical and psychological weakness and narrow-mindedness, she has been continually violated and mortified by practices such as circumcision, infibulation and force-feeding, supposedly justified in an essentially 'phallocentric' society by the need to restrain her 'natural inclination' to be unfaithful.

Elsewhere (Chapter 5) the alleged predisposition of the female sex to infidelity is discussed. It is the extent to which practices such as circumcision and infibulation reflect the fact that in such societies marriage makes women the possession of men that concerns us here. Amongst the Moors of Mauritania and northern Mali, a man's social standing can be measured by his wife's waistline so he tries to increase it by force-feeding her. A few years ago, a Moor appeared in court in Gao, Mali, accused of having killed his wife by suffocation while force-feeding her. Undoubtedly grieved by the loss of his wife, the man denied the charge, claiming that he had sacrificed her to a tradition going back in the mists of time only in order to increase her beauty.

But such examples of male domination seem to belong to traditional African culture and appear to be giving way as literacy and urbanisation spread. *Lovelaw* chose Egypt as a country where the influence and values of Islam mingle with the forces of growth, economic development and industrialisation. At corner news-stands in Cairo can be bought any one of a hundred Muslim tracts on all manner of issues relating to the roles of men and women, the effects of change and the moral implications of such questions as women working and premarital sex. Traditional Muslim teaching insists that the right place for the woman, the only place for the woman to practise her main task of being a wife and mother, is the home.

In a typical fundamentalist tract entitled *Problems Facing the Modern Muslim Woman*, Islamic writer Ibrahim Mahmoud El Gamal confronts the problem of infanticide involving girls.

Islam, he protests, has never sanctioned the practice but prohibits the crime and insists that men and women have the same rights. Islam has also demolished the custom which forced girls to marry without their approval. 'But as Islam guaranteed the woman her rights,' he continues, 'it also required her to carry out her duties towards her husband.' And these duties, quite simply, are loyalty, love, respect and obedience with regard to a number of prohibitions. The true Muslim woman is not allowed to go out without her husband's permission, is not allowed to admit strangers to the house in his absence, is not allowed to give voluntarily from the household's finances without his approval and has no right to refuse his sexual demands without lawful reason. Her duty, quite simply, is to manage the house while his duty is to manage her and protect and support her and their children.

Such traditional views live uneasily beside the same employment trends that are underway in the US and Europe. More and more Egyptian women in the urban areas are going out to work. Dia Amr illustrates the situation perfectly. Not quite sixteen, the legal age of marriage, when her mother spotted thirty-year-old Dr Mustapha Fahim as a potential husband, Dia Amr married him three days after her sixteenth birthday. She hardly knew him. The marriage was arranged via her parents, his parents and Dr Fahim himself. The contract had a business air to it, sealing two families as much as two individuals together. For Dr Fahim, a former world-class Egyptian boxer, the roles of husband and wife in marriage are clear, distinct and complementary. His wife's responsibility, like that of Mrs Fujisawa in Kyoto, is the home. His responsibility is everything else. But Dia Amr works outside the family home. Hers is an eight-hour day working as a tourist guide showing visitors around the Sphinx and explaining some of her country's remarkable history. She enjoys her work and both welcome the extra income.

But such a demanding job produces stresses. Sometimes Dr Fahim comes home in the evening to find the dinner unprepared or the housework not done. He points out the deficiencies and insists that they be put right. Taking tourists around the Sphinx is one thing, but there are priorities, and Dia Amr's are the household – and her husband.

And Dia Amr – what does this liberated lady make of her irritable husband and his domestic criticisms?

> Well, of course, sometimes I think he is right but I feel that I cannot help it because I am so exhausted by my job and it is too much for me to come back in the evenings and still work in the house. But I calm him down and try to do my best but actually in most cases it is too much for me. Sometimes I have a sense of guilt but it cannot be helped. I do sometimes think that he should give me a hand instead of just criticising. But then I say that the tradition here in Egypt is that the man is always the boss and wants everything to be done for him. In fact my husband does give a hand when other men don't. So I feel satisfied.

Not merely does Dia Amr accept the traditional view of the respective roles of man and woman within the Egyptian marriage, but following a pilgrimage to Mecca she has taken to wearing the veil and long dresses. The veil, admittedly, is but a partial one which covers her hair and permits her to carry out her tour guide duties unimpeded but her decision nevertheless is a significant one. She has made it only partly out of respect for her husband and as a guarantee that her beauty is for his eyes alone. Her main motive is religious.

These traditional values are transmitted to their children. Their eldest son, Muhammad, is about to get engaged. Dia, for all her complaints about fatigue and exhaustion as she battles to cope with two jobs, insists that Muhammad too should be the boss in his own home, the one who makes the final decisions, whose wife shall be a loyal, obedient and faithful servant.

Amina el-Said is the first woman journalist in Egypt and has the longest-running letters column in a monthly news magazine. She bases her opinions on the thousands of letters she's been receiving over the years from both men and women, and she writes regularly on the challenges Egypt faces as it wrestles with Islamic fundamentalism and Western values. First, she is critical of the kind of man that traditional Egyptian society fosters. What she terms 'the arrogance of the Arab man' leads him to seek superiority in everything. The cause of this superiority complex she attributes to the upbringing of children in the Arab world. When children are small parents are invariably more tolerant of the boy,

> If the girl complains of this preference, they say, 'No, he is a boy, you are a girl.' They are always saying that at every age. When they are teenagers the

boy goes out a lot. If the girl wants to go out a lot they say, 'No, you can't do that because you are a girl and he is a boy.' They are always reminding the girl that she is an inferior creature and that is the real problem in our country – and not only in our country but all over the East.

But, and it is a big but, Amina el-Said is not at all sure that she wants Egypt to proceed along the road to so-called emancipation. She is especially critical of Western marriage which seems to her to be a sort of retirement. In Egypt, she points out, marriage is the start of adult life. Both spouses commence life together and negotiate joy, sadness, happiness and heartbreak, satisfaction and dissatisfaction together. Together they get to know each other and themselves. In the West, young people of both sexes fraternise together, somewhat promiscuously to Egyptian eyes, and then, having satisfied their desire for freedom and for novelty, they 'retire' into marriage. According to Amina el-Said, women in the West are under immense pressure to turn themselves into men!

In Hungary, however, the State struggles to turn men into women, or at least into participants in the domestic tasks of housekeeping and child-rearing, by teaching teenage boys how to change nappies, while primary-school children are encouraged to write essays on the similarities of the activities performed in the home by their Daddies and Mummies.

In a report in 1980 to the National Council of Hungarian Women, the President, Mrs Laszlo Erdei, noted the disadvantageous earning position of women – the earnings of 50 per cent of women were under 3000 forint (£43) a month while only 14 per cent of men belonged to this category, while in the highest wage and salary category there were four times as many men as women. But she detected a considerable improvement throughout the 1970s. There had been a welcome expansion in the network of child-care institutions so that in 1980 15 per cent of all children up to three years of age could be accommodated in day nurseries along with 85 per cent of the three- to six-year-olds. But it is Mrs Erdei's statement concerning the change of attitude amongst young married couples that is particularly noteworthy,

Young husbands are far more helpful with the housework, sharing with the wife's 'second shift' at home. With the older generation, the situation is different: there the largest share of household duties falls upon the woman.

In these families, a fair division of labour is far more difficult to bring about than in young families.

However, there is disagreement about the extent to which there are genuine changes in behaviour concerning roles within and outside the Hungarian home. *Lovelaw* filmed the recording of a scene from Hungary's hugely popular radio serial, 'The Szabo Family', a sort of everyday story of city folk, similar to Britain's long-running 'The Archers'. The episode featured married heroine Manci complaining bitterly to her taxi-driver husband Laci that she had to do two jobs, her work in the factory and her work as a wife, servant and mother of their daughter, Janika. 'But you are the mother,' protests Laci after losing a feeble argument to the effect that occasionally he helps. After all, he adds, he needs to sleep at home to regenerate the strength he expends all night behind the wheel of his taxi. Manci, however, has spent all night organising the factory brigade and her patience snaps,

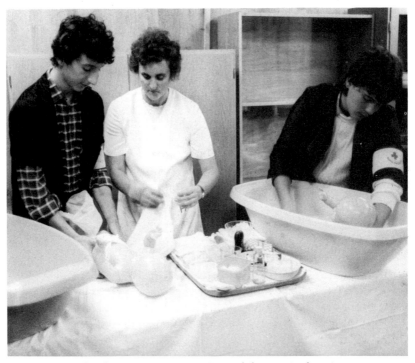

A technical school in Eger, Hungary. Part of the curriculum is a course on health care in which, amongst other things, the boys are taught how to look after babies

Have you by any chance ever heard something about the fair distribution of burdens? Have you heard why we women had to be emancipated? So that we are not just to work at home for the family. So that with hard work we should be able to make money as well. When did you last cook us lunch? When did you last work the washing machine? When did you bring home enough money to be able to tell me, 'You just stay home, Manci. Be nothing more, just wife and mother; be a housewife, be pretty, well-groomed, desirable – leave all the rest to me. I will do the rest'? Have you ever said that? Are we equal? Yes we are. All right then, you get up, do the washing, make lunch while *I* sleep.

The marriage of Piroska and Lajos Pozsik bears some resemblance to the Szabos'. The Pozsiks have been married for sixteen years and have two children. Piroska works as a psychiatric nurse in Eger's large psychiatric hospital. Her husband works as a driver of road repairing machinery. The first few years of their marriage were spent living with Lajos's mother. Then they purchased a plot for 33,000 forints (£480) (his mother provided 20,000 (£300)) and over a ten-year period built their own home. Piroska gets up before 5 am, works until 2 pm, then shops locally and is home by 3.30 pm. She then cooks, cleans, washes and when the children return from school she feeds them and helps with their homework. When Lajos arrives home from his twelve-hour shift his dinner is ready.

There is no true equality, Piroska insists, whatever is said about the State-backed policy. Why doesn't her husband help?

Because this is how he was brought up. It is all a matter of upbringing. How shall I put it, he was brought up that everything was done for him. And this upbringing shows now. And he never got used to it so that when we moved here I started to do everything myself. If he finds a plate here in the sink he will not wash it. He will wait for me.

Lajos spends his free time reading the newspaper, drinking with his friends and providing fervent and constant support for the local Eger football team at their twice-weekly matches. His adjournments to a local café to engage in lengthy post-match analyses is a particular bone of contention between the couple. Piroska also worries that her husband's obvious unwillingness to pull his domestic weight will influence her son, Peter, who will grow up with the same view of male and female roles as that of his father.

For Lajos there is no problem defining the sex roles. His work takes precedence for the very good reason that his earnings exceed those of his wife. As for doing domestic work in the house, this might interfere with the occasional moonlighting job and would make little financial sense. He is impatient with Piroska's complaining, scolding, and lecturing about his behaviour and his lack of domesticity. After all, he objects, he works the longer hours and he earns more per hour worked. As for all the sloganising about equal pay for equal work, he has little time for it,

No woman can ever accomplish as much as a man. She will never make as much money as a man, not with physical labour anyway. This equality simply means that they are equal all right because we lift them up. We do appreciate them, we lift them up, we love them. But that they are worth the same when it comes to any kind of work? It is not that they cannot perform well enough, but when it comes to stamina, well they are not in the same league! We respect, love, appreciate them. They bear and bring up the kids, they are in charge of the household. But then our mothers used to do all these things just as well. And yet they used to come second. Now women come first. Their word matters more. They are the bosses in the home needless to say, materially, forint-wise and all. Isn't that enough for them?

In other parts of the world, such as North America and Scandinavia, it is by no means enough. Compared with most other countries, Sweden has made considerable progress in the field of equal opportunities pursued on the basis of the unashamedly individualistic belief that everyone, regardless of sex, must be able to develop and participate in all aspects of community life according to their capabilities. Swedes deploy two words to express the idea of equality: *jämlikhet* and *jämställdhet*. The former can adequately be translated as equality – the philosophical or ethical principle of the equal worth of every human being regardless of sex, creed or ethnic background. The latter refers to equivalent conditions, opportunities and responsibilities for all, women and men. Sweden simply insists that whatever the biological and behavioural differences, men and women should be entitled to the same practical opportunities in family life, working life and society.

One of the main thrusts of legislative reform in the 1970s was to eradicate the principle of the man as the chief wage-earner in the family. Individual income taxation for everyone was introduced in 1971 and led to a rapid increase in the extent to which women sought gainful employment. Nevertheless, a large share in the increase was in part-time rather than full-time work, a trend which has continued in Sweden to the present day.

So, reflecting the view that the roots of inequality lie in early development and training, Swedish social engineers turned their attention to education. The new compulsory curriculum which came into force in the 1982–3 school year is more specifically concerned than its predecessor with giving boys and girls identical education. Home economics and technology are compulsory for all children at junior level. Handicraft is the same for all pupils throughout their school career.

Despite changes in attitudes, behaviour remains remarkably resistant to reform. In one widely publicised survey in Sweden, teachers were called upon to divide their time equally between boys and girls. Although under supervision, teachers devoted 70 per cent of their time to boys and yet the boys still felt unfairly treated and believed that the girls were getting too much attention. The practical realities of Swedish education are difficult to alter, too. Ninety per cent of head teachers are male whereas practically all dining-room and office staff are women. Teachers of younger children are mostly women while older children are taught by men. Only 1 per cent of junior level teachers are male while 65 per cent of intermediate level teachers are female. In contrast, women constituted only 18 per cent of PhD students in 1982 and in the same year only 5 per cent of university and college professors and 34 per cent of assistant professors were women.

But the Swedes refuse to countenance defeat. In 1974 they introduced a parental insurance scheme entitling both parents to share leave of absence in connection with childbirth. In 1975 they introduced new abortion legislation which entitles women to decide for themselves up to and including the eighteenth week of pregnancy. In 1979 new legislation permitted parents to work a six-hour day. In 1982 came a supplementary pension for those who care for children at home. In 1984 an equal opportunities policy was made mandatory for the national sector.

Elsewhere (Chapter 7), I discuss these innovative policies in greater detail. For the moment it is worth noting the extent to

which the Swedes are beginning to acknowledge that no significant change in the role and status of women can be achieved
without comparable modifications of the relevant attitudes
held by men and, more importantly, of the relevant behaviours
in which they indulge.

Which brings us back to Mrs A, with whom we began. Her
symptoms and her role conflict are clearly shared to varying
extents by Mrs Fujisawa in Kyoto, Piroska Pozsik in Eger and
Dia Amr in Cairo. They are all straining to cope with the fact
that emancipation means two jobs and the taking on of 'male'
responsibilities without relinquishing many 'female' ones. Mr
A, for his part, is a member of that club, fellow membership of
which is certainly open to Mr Fujisawa, Lajos Pozsik and Dr
Fahim, seeing that anyone can qualify as long as a) he is male, b)
he regards housework as 'women's work', and c) he does as
little of it as is possible.

Throughout the developed world, and detectable in various
parts of the developing world, can be seen obvious trends. An
increasing number of women, young and old, single and married, educated and uneducated, are seeking gainful
employment outside the home. Many do so for financial
reasons, many for reasons of personal development and satisfaction, many for a mixture of both. The predominantly male
world outside the home has extended a somewhat lukewarm
welcome and has made it plain that only to a limited extent will
such a trend be encouraged. Women will be paid the same as
men only when, on relatively rare occasions, one of their
number makes it to the top. Otherwise they will be paid less, in
view of the fact that in general out of necessity, rather than
preference, they seek part-time work. They have domestic
responsibilities and the work they do, by virtue of the fact that it
is done by women, is seen as inherently less valuable.

On these terms, it is not easy to believe that women have
greatly benefited from moving outside the home and into a
'man's world'. One consequence has been a revival of enthusi-
asm, particularly among male commentators, for the Victorian
ideal of the home, that 'haven in a heartless world', as the American commentator on personal values, Christopher Lasch, has
ironically termed it, a refuge where women can find in faithful
devotion to those they love the meaning of and justification for

the inhumanity, the competitiveness and ruthlessness of the working lives of their men. Within such a conception of the family, relationships are seen as warm, spiritual, caring and spontaneous. Within such a family, man and wife conspire to give meaning to their lives. Within such a family, men deal with things, women with feelings. Though women have taken on extra work to sustain the family financially, they are held as responsible as ever for upholding loving relationships. In such circumstances, it is hardly surprising, though the evidence is inadequate, that contemporary social afflictions, such as violence, delinquency, hooliganism and juvenile crime, are from time to time blamed on working mothers, implicitly or explicitly, betraying their fundamental duty.

But there can be no going back to the Victorian family ideal for the simple reason that more and more people, men as well as women, see such a conception of family and marital life as inappropriate and even oppressive. Peter Marris, a sociologist with a particular interest in the relationship between personal and public life, makes the point succinctly,

> The rationalism of scientific management denies the validity of personal affection and loyalties in most of the work that men do, while the idealisation of domesticity denies the validity of rational self-interest in a woman's management of her mothering. Men want the chance to be loving and women to be self-interested, so that both can find themselves in some meaningful structure of relationships. But each seems to threaten the other, as men fear that feminists want to drag the only relationships uncontaminated by buying and selling into the market-place of professional child care, wages for housework, and take-home fast foods; and women that men, once again, are undermining sexual equality by their age-old romance with mothering.[6]

The problem seems to be that the economic pressures to support and fulfil women's aspirations of self-interest, the economic recession notwithstanding, appear very much stronger than any equivalent pressure to endorse men's desire to be loving. The first stage of the revolution, namely the penetration of male citadels of power, while far from complete, is at least underway, in Islamic Egypt and communist Hungary, in capitalist America and socialist Sweden. But the transformation of male values is still just an idea in the writings of such feminists as Betty Friedan and Marilyn French, although the tentative social initiatives of Scandinavia do suggest that it is being taken seriously.

In the meantime, the accusation made by Egypt's Amina el-Said that Western women are being forced to become like men retains an uncomfortable grain of truth. Should such a situation persist and the second stage of the revolution, if that is what it is, be aborted or stillborn, then what becomes of man's need of woman and woman's of man? If women can manage perfectly well without having men to earn and care for them, and if men can no longer justify their role as carers for wife and family, what becomes of marriage? Does it lose its tension, its passion, its fire? Does it become more a companionship and less a relationship of need? In this relationship of equals what is the emotional glue, now that economic dependency and patriarchal authority have been or are in the process of being overthrown? And what of the children?

4 PARENTS AND CHILDREN

The fact that my wife and I have seven children provokes incredulity and curiosity from those puzzled to know why we have chosen to sustain a Kenyan-sized family in a country where 1·8 children per couple is the norm. After we have gently demurred from any suggestion that the size of our family was the Pope of Rome's choice rather than our own (an understandable red herring given our Irish, Roman Catholic background) and pointed out that we actually like children and find the presence of several brothers and sisters makes the task of rearing them easier than when there are just two or three, our interrogators tend to lose interest and begin to provide reasons for their own relative restraint. Top of the list is cost. Indeed, on the basis of what I must confess is a somewhat personal and scientifically unrepresentative sample of cocktail-party interviews, many women and not a few men in middle-class Britain today would like to have more children (although not necessarily as many as we have) but just cannot afford it.

Having a child in Britain today does appear to be an expensive business. According to the magazine *Parents*, the initial cost of a first child could be as high as £9849, assuming the parents bought everything they needed new. An examination of a table of expenses published by *The Times* reveals that the single most costly expense is listed under 'Hidden Extras' and these include 'loss of wife's earnings'. (See opposite.)

The arrival of effective contraception has helped release women from their former social destiny of child-rearing and domestic work and has enabled them to extend themselves in other directions – to acquire careers, attend meetings, obtain higher education – in the words of feminist commentator Debbie Taylor writing in *Women: A World Report*,[1] 'to stretch a hand into the worlds that men have occupied freely for so long'. But, she adds, the price of that freedom is often the sacrifice of a wanted child. Having said that, modern contraception has finally broken the link between sex and procreation and it is estimated that about half the women in the world who want to stop having children temporarily or permanently are now able to fulfil that wish. Throughout the developed world, birth rates have fallen steadily and in some countries anxiety is growing lest the population fails to replace itself and society ends up with too many old people and insufficient young and middle-aged to sustain them.

The reasons why couples, when given the choice, decide not to have children cast a revealing light on why we choose to have children in the first place. Until recently, analysis of this choice was confined to abstract and academic journals. Conventional wisdom declares that couples have children as naturally as cats have kittens. It is the way things are. The belief that a couple does not become a family until there are children is epitomised in the phrase 'starting a family'.

Important the family may be but in a consumer-oriented society children (at an initial cost of £9849) take their place beside higher degrees, two incomes, cars, washing machines, video recorders, holidays abroad and a bigger mortgage in the

THE COST OF A FIRST BABY			
	1984	1985	CHANGE 1984–5 £ per cent
	£	£	
Maternity clothes	100	141	+41
Baby clothes	118	133	+12
Baby equipment	483	570	+18
Nursery preparation	71	85	+20
Baby food	190	201	+6
Heating and toiletries	153	163	+6.5
Nappies	318	331	+4
Incidentals	256	292	+14
Hidden extras (inc. loss of wife's earnings)	6470	7920	+22
Fares	10	12.50	+25
Total	8169	9849	+20.5
Less allowances and savings	−1050	−1128	+7.5
Total costs	7119	8721	+22.5

list of priorities faced by the average couple. This unromantic fact underpins in one way or another the efforts by governments and international agencies to persuade countries with booming or persistently high birth rates to reduce their fertility. 'Development is the best contraceptive,' was the slogan of the First World Population Conference in 1974, emphasising the fact that under affluent conditions many satisfactions, such as those parents derive from the achievements of their children, are more likely to be derived when parents invest in fewer rather than more offspring.

However, as American demographer Ronald Freeman points out, fertility declines have also taken place in a number of countries such as Sri Lanka, Thailand, Indonesia and China, where there has as yet been limited development and where the populations remain overwhelmingly poor and rural. The reasons lie in a number of trends which such societies have in common including,

1 The achievement of better health and longer life, which means fewer births are needed for the survival of any desired number. This encourages investment in the future.

2 The spread of higher education for both boys and girls increases the costs and decreases the benefits of large families while children are in school; fewer, better educated children may provide greater satisfaction than more, poorly educated ones.

3 The introduction of welfare institutions which provide minimum subsistence for the masses, at least in food, has decreased dependence on children.

4 The improvement of communication and transportation facilities to provide more information, services and goods.

The last factor may be crucially important. Through the means of mass communication, particularly television, available throughout the Third World, increasing numbers of people have become aware of alternatives to their life-styles and have begun to aspire to something different, even though these aspirations are often poorly defined. And as the boons and benefits, the trinkets and the trash of the modern consumer society filter their way into the developing world villages, they change the lives of those who have them and the larger number of people who want them.

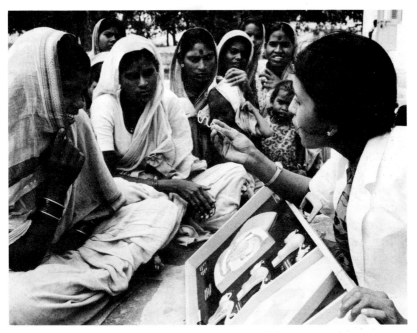

Family planning in India has been most successful in areas where women are well educated. In the cities many couples now restrict themselves to having just two children

And so the decision to have a child, be it in Madurai or Manchester, Eger or Edgbaston, is a finely balanced one involving debits and credits. For a rural population in the Philippines, 75 per cent of the costs of rearing a third child comes from buying goods and services, the remaining 25 per cent comes from costs in time (or lost wages). But receipts from child earnings, work at home and old-age support offset 46 per cent of the total. The remaining 54 per cent, that is, the net cost of the child, is equivalent to about 6 per cent of a father's annual earnings. Teenagers in this society contribute as much to the household cash income as do adults. In addition, much of women's traditional work, such as tilling the land and harvesting crops, craftwork and retailing, can be combined with looking after children.

Contrast such a state of affairs with urban America. A study of family life there in 1960 showed that almost 50 per cent of the costs of a third child are time costs while receipts from the child offset only 4 per cent of the costs. Neither do children contribute much to household chores. One US study found that children aged between twelve and seventeen spent less than an hour a day doing housework, and those between six and eleven spent under half an hour a day. The only surprising thing to me about such figures is that they seem a little high!

High infant and child mortality is another reason why couples in the developing world persist in reproducing. One-twelfth of the world's babies die within the first year of life. In many parts of sub-Saharan Africa the figure is one in five and in much of India, Bangladesh and Pakistan it is one in seven. In such countries parents understandably feel the need to ensure that some children survive, and in those societies where boys have a higher social status than girls parents may need to have as many as five children to ensure that at least one son survives to adult life.

In some societies there are traditions which depend on there being children to carry them out. There is, for example, a Brahmin tradition that when a father reaches his sixtieth birthday, the children and grandchildren gather together and the couple repeat their marriage ceremony surrounded by their offspring – the *Shasthi Abtha Poorthi*. S. Raghavan reached his sixtieth birthday after forty-one years of marriage. At his *Shasthi Abtha Poorthi*, he and his wife were joined by their four children and nine grandchildren. It is regarded as important that children witness their parents' marriage so that they can show their respect, regard and love. From that marriage has come their life, their education, their employment, their own families.

There is a Hindu belief that an individual's soul is only released after death if certain religious rites are performed, including the eldest son setting fire to the funeral pyre of his father or mother. Ramamurti and his wife Kamambal are childless after thirty years of marriage. Both are in their fifties and so the possibility that they will produce a child has gone. They have approached two of Ramamurti's brothers with a view to adopting one of their sons but to no avail. A man without a child is condemned to spend eternity in a Hindu version of hell. It is therefore permitted that a man without a child can take another wife with the permission of the wife he already has. It is an intriguing form of surrogacy in which the surrogate mother is added to the existing family. Sadly, however, on occasions the childless wife is ejected from the family home in favour of the new wife.

Most people want to leave something in life after they die. Thus do the children and grandchildren at the Indian re-marriage ceremony reflect and represent their nation's buoyant birth rate. More prosaic explanations are forthcoming too. In societies such as India, with high infant mortality, there is anxiety about who will look after people when they are old and ill. Ironically, this is one anxiety which is not eliminated by affluence. In the developed world, where the proportion of the population over the age of sixty-five is in excess of 15 per cent and where the average family size is less than two children, we also worry about who will care for us when we are old and grey and full of sleep and nodding by the fire. In countries such as India, Indonesia, Korea, the Philippines and Turkey, over 90 per cent of parents anticipate their children will support them in old age. Such countries look askance at the West where, allegedly, we condemn our aged parents to dismal, institu-tional lives in old people's homes and long-stay hospitals. In fact, notwithstanding Britain's Welfare State and its 'cradle to the grave' philosophy, it is children and not the State which here too provide the overwhelming bulk of support for old peo-ple. Only 2 per cent of the elderly live in residential institu-tions and only 10 per cent are likely to enter a residential home at any stage in their lives. However, a significant difference between India and Britain is that in India one of the explicit motives for having children is to guarantee this later support; in Britain, if such a motive plays a role it is largely a subconscious one. In India, the public portrayal of the tradition of children caring for their elderly relatives is as a duty and an honour. In Britain and many other developed countries, it is often envis-aged as a burden.

Likewise, having children can be seen largely as burden-some. With economic and particularly educational develop-ment, many women now *expect* to work and *elect* to have children. In some instances, a woman and her work may well be tied by a bond of personal satisfaction which is stronger and more real than the mixed blessing at the end of the umbilical cord. Childbirth and the period immediately after it are portrayed as a time of tension, strain and marital disharmony. In my personal experience and in my work as a psychiatrist I am confronted by how often parenthood is a time not of new opportunities but new isolation. It occurs most commonly when the father is in mid-career and preoccupied with ambitions and self-doubts which he seeks to relieve in domestic bliss. This, however, can be hard to come by with sleepless nights, nappies, chaos and a chronically tired partner unable to fathom quite why the baby does not match with those bonny portraits in the women's magazines and the benign descriptions in the many available self-help baby guides. Alone all day with the baby, the mother makes more emotional demands on her partner than ever before and often at a time when he feels most in need of a listening ear himself. And there goes the baby again, crying despite feed and dry nappy. Sometimes I am not surprised that there is so much physical abuse directed against children under three nor that this is the peak season for divorce; and particularly when you consider that much of this early exposure to the delights and travails of child-rearing occurs with the new parents bereft of the kind of family and communal support that characterises family life in Third World villages.

Yet such a gloomy picture, perhaps derived from too long a clinical exposure to psychopathology, should not obscure the fact that, for the most part, those children who are born appear wanted. But there is a much more cold-blooded economic reckoning involved than is often admitted. It changes with the number of children in the family. Studies of mothers in the US, the Philippines and Korea indicate that economic and emotional factors operate in all three societies but economic considerations are clearly more important in the Philippines (where fertility is higher), whereas concern with the restrictions children place on parents is clearly greatest in the US. In all three countries, couples demonstrate a change in the values they emphasise as their families grow. The first child is important because of its role in cementing the marriage and for bringing the spouses closer together as well as providing someone to carry on the family name. Couples also stress the desire to have someone to love and care for and to bring play and fun into their lives.

In considering a second child, parents emphasise the desire for a companion for their first child. They also place weight on the desire for a child of the opposite sex from the first. Similar values are prominent in relation to third, fourth and fifth children; emphasis is also given to the pleasure derived from watching the children grow. After the fifth child, economic considerations predominate. Parents speak of sixth and later children in terms of their helping around the house, contributing to the support of the household and providing for security in old age. For first to third children, parental time taken away from work and other pursuits is the main drawback. For fourth and later children, the direct financial burden is more prominent.

The experience of Hungary illustrates the impact of industrialisation, the growth of educational opportunities and the problems of rapid urbanisation on a nation's birth rate and the oscillations in national policy as it struggles to reconcile the individual's choice to have or not have children with the greater communal good. In the 1870s and 1880s, Hungary's birth rate was high by European standards, at about forty-five live births per 1000 inhabitants, a rate equivalent to that in Africa at the present time. Before the First World War it had fallen to about thirty, after the Second World War to about twenty and by the mid-1960s, following the introduction in 1956 of a particularly liberal abortion law, it had fallen to 12·9, one of the lowest rates in Europe.

In 1973, the Hungarian government, alarmed at the fall and its implications for the nation's ability to maintain its numbers, instituted a series of incentives for child-raising. The government raised the amount provided to mothers for child benefit and pumped extra money into the house-building programme. The birth rate rose marginally but by 1980 it had fallen again to 12·6 births per 1000 inhabitants. By this time, a similar picture was apparent in most of the countries of Europe, East as well as West.

Population surveys in Hungary confirm the extent to which the norm of the small family has become entrenched. In 1977, out of every 100 people planning to get married, seventy-four planned to have no more than two children, hardly any planned to have no children, hardly any planned to have more than two children. In 1949, the average number of children in families was over two; by 1970 it had fallen to 1·67; by 1980 to 1·62. According to the census data of 1980 only 8 per cent of Hungarian women had borne four or more children.

Explanations put forward for this low birth rate are numerous. They include the catastrophic housing situation, the fall in the number of marriages, the rise in divorce, the changed role of women in Hungarian society, the economic recession, the high abortion rate, an imbalance in the age structure and the break-up of the family as a unit.

The Hungarian housing situation is certainly the most obvious deterrent to the formation of harmonious family life. While the situation has improved over the years (from a ratio of 265 inhabitants per 100 rooms in 1949 to 142 per 100 rooms in 1983), it is still very difficult. Little more than half of apartments are fully equipped with modern conveniences, less than one in seven have central heating and close to 50 per cent have no toilet facilities. It has been estimated that 40 per cent of the disagreements that lead families to break up are caused by unresolved housing problems. At the present time, 52 per cent of all married couples in Budapest live with their parents compared with 13 per cent a generation ago. Only 11 per cent of all young couples are allocated a local council apartment compared with 42 per cent a generation ago.

An intriguing government incentive to couples to produce children involves the provision of favourable loans. Young couples who promise to have two children have 30,000 forints (£433) per child, that is 60,000 forints (£866) in all deducted from any repayments to the Hungarian National Savings Bank (Országos Takarék Pénztár) on any loans they take out to set up house. This is equivalent to a 10 per cent reduction on the average price of a Hungarian apartment. In the event of failure

---

But why do these women accept the role of mother? Perhaps because they feel their lives would be unbearably empty without children? Or, perhaps, for many people, this is the relatively easy way of getting an apartment? In other words, do they interpret the new life as a means of payment? People who are not yet mature enough for motherhood or fatherhood would like to build their own existence, but they have no money in their pockets to pay sums in six figures for an apartment, so they pay with their sons or daughters. The after-effects of a well-intended family policy are the OTP children who are often treated as part of a building.

*Article in a
Hungarian labour union daily*

> We are gathered here to celebrate a real festival of joy. Every infant means hope and promise, the fruit of life's creative forces, the guarantee that life continues. That is why people smile when they see an infant. The warmth of love makes faces beautiful; people think of the future but they remember their own good or bad but by all means dear childhood too. Children mean happiness for parents and relatives too. A child is a new branch on the trunk of the family; deep love and dreams usher him in. It is only the mother who really knows that although according to the course of nature something extraordinary happens. With the arrival of the child, the life of the family feels more complete; the little nest has become more friendly and more intimate and cosy. Husband and wife are closer to each other in a family where life is accompanied by the music of laughter, babble and crying. The joy of the individual and the smaller community is harmoniously joined by the joy of the larger community. Every healthy society is filled with joy by the expectation of new life, the birth of an infant. In our homeland, where socialism is being built, where the relationship between individual and community, family and society has become very close, interests are identical and mothers and families are taken eminently good care of.
>
> Gabriella Gazdag,
> District Council Registrar
> officiating at a Hungarian
> name-giving ceremony

to produce the promised child or children or in the case of divorce the money has to be repaid. What happens if the unfortunate couple is infertile is curiously neglected.

However, this example of a novel law to influence the development of a family is not without its hazards. Hungarians have become familiar with a new group of children said to be virtually predestined from birth to become juvenile delinquents – the so-called 'OTP' children, named after the initials of the Bank which provides the monetary incentives. Not all those who promise to have children are suited for the role of parenthood and, it is said, that the price of an apartment is paid with children who are treated as an economic commodity.

In recent years, gynaecologists have reported an increase in the number of women having 'imaginary' or phantom pregnancies. The symptoms are those of a real pregnancy and in many cases it is only in the maternity clinic that the truth is revealed.

'In nearly every case,' declares a report in *Magyar Nemzet*, the daily of the Patriotic People's Front, 'all the mothers were married, lived in local council or in their own apartments, and all received an official allowance of 60,000 forints [£866].' Their one wish was to fulfil the conditions even to the extent of an imaginary conception!

The Hungarian authorities struggle in other ways to redress the population balance which it clearly perceives as having gone too far in the opposite direction. The benefits of child-bearing are extolled particularly at name-giving ceremonies, the secular baptism, which often take place within a company or industrial setting and which give the State an opportunity to congratulate parents on doing their duty by society. More concrete benefits are provided too. If a woman has three children, the total amount of State benefits is equivalent to a full adult wage. Her job is guaranteed with all annual increments and full pension rights protected. Mothers have special 'mother's day' holidays – three per child per year – and paid leave whenever any of their children fall ill.

Yet the low fertility persists. A crucial factor, probably as important as the housing shortage, is the increasing role played by women in the economy. Women are taking over more and more positions and are spending less time bringing up families. Eighty-one per cent of women aged between fifteen and fifty-four are employed compared with 85 per cent of men in the same age-group. Women in Hungary can be found in virtually every field of physical activity while in certain 'feminine' occupations, such as hairdressing, nursing, weaving and waitressing, they occupy 90 per cent of the positions. Fifty-eight per cent of white-collar workers are women, 59 per cent of administrators and 92 per cent of subordinate administrators. Whereas in 1960, 46 per cent of women with children chose to stay at home, this proportion has steadily fallen – 23 per cent in 1970, 11 per cent in 1980 – and the attractions of and need to work for women are proving major disincentives to having children.

If governments in the more affluent parts of the world struggle with scant success to invent ways to persuade women to have larger families, how successful is government pressure, legislation and persuasion in the opposite direction in the developing world? Variable, would appear to be the answer. Half of the developing world's population is currently below reproductive age and the imbalance between births and deaths is now so large that whatever steps are taken global population will continue to grow until well into the next century. The difficulties faced by the Kenyan government, the converse of those being wrestled with by the Hungarians, dramatically illustrate the problem. Over the past forty years, the number of children borne by the average woman during her reproductive life (the total fertility rate) actually rose from 6·1 in 1941 to 8·1 in 1979. The population of Kenya, estimated to be a mere 2 million in 1900, reached 4 million in 1940, 8 million in 1960 and 16 million in 1980! While the crude birth rate has scarcely risen since 1940, the crude death rate has fallen sharply. The consequence is that in terms of school provision alone, Kenya's spiralling numbers require the annual building of 1300 new classrooms for first-year primary-school children alone.

At a school in the Vihiga district, the Kenyan region that has the highest birth rate in the country that has the highest birth rate in the world, the teacher, Mrs Edith Eboi, begins a reading lesson with her pupils. The government-provided textbook tells of a happy three-child family – the class, made up of children from families that average eight in number, listen attentively. Back at Mrs Eboi's house, we learn why the government's earnest intentions are still largely frustrated. Mrs Eboi and her husband explain that when they were younger they knew nothing of contraception. The way to win respect and achieve social standing was to produce as many children as possible. Mr Joshua Eboi feels the value of his life is determined by the number of children he has and he works hard in order to pass on his ways to the youngsters, 'So that the next time they will be proud and say, "My father did this for me and I must do this for my children."'

Despite the influence of tribal elders who insist that it is 'better to die than to cease to bear children', there are signs that Kenyan women, particularly in the cities, are beginning to doubt the wisdom of large families. Rosemary Eboi, the eldest of her parents' eight children, plans to have only two children of her own. For her, such practical considerations as inflation, the price of clothes, home utensils and education, and the

Above. *Women at a children's clinic in the Vihiga district of Kenya.*
Right. *In the same area Mrs Edith Eboi teaches her young pupils at the local school. Vihiga has the highest birth rate in Kenya but the women there, and elsewhere in Kenya, would like smaller families*

problem of finding a sufficiently spacious house means that 'there are many things to consider before having a whole row of kids'.

On a hotel terrace overlooking Lake Victoria, a group of married men sit talking with *Lovelaw* about Kenya's remarkable fertility. John Agola has seventeen children and feels he should have thirty if he is to be able to fight to obtain the land such a tribe deserves. Joshua Ogadho has ten children, admits that this is probably too many and blames the excess on the fact that he has several wives. The men argue over the right number of children Kenyan parents should have but all are agreed that contraception is unwise. The pill, they say, causes bleeding, deformities, mutant babies with two heads. Contraception in general leads to promiscuity and prostitution. They are also agreed about why they, as men, desire more children. It is for social reasons. Men who have a large number of children are respected. Conversely, men who have a small number are belittled.

Florence Malande, a family-planning counsellor in Vihiga, confirms that the rumours of side-effects and the much-heralded dangers of female promiscuity have affected birth-control practice in the country. There are rumours, she points out, that 'if you use the coil it will run up to the heart, it will run up to the back, it will run up to the head'. In addition to questions of social status, the anxiety concerning infant mortality still motivates couples to have more children than they can manage and the nation can afford. As for Mrs Malande herself – she has seven children!

Take-up rates of available methods of contraception vary greatly from country to country. One important factor is the extent to which governments involve themselves in what is one of the most personal of decisions. According to the 1984 World Development Report, approximately eighty-five countries in the developing world, representing about 95 per cent of the population, now provide some form of support to family-planning programmes. However, virtually every programme fails to reach most rural people while even in the towns and cities the quality of the services is poor and discontinuation

rates are high. Of the twenty-seven countries in the developing world which have yet to introduce a family-planning programme, almost half are in Africa, where incomes are the lowest in the world, population growth is the highest and the potential impact of family planning may well be greatest.

The percentage take-up by married women of contraception varies greatly between the developed and the developing worlds, and within the developing world. In China, Hong Kong and Singapore, nearly 70 per cent of women in the reproductive phase of their life use contraception, a proportion as high as that in the US and Western Europe. The proportion in Latin America is around 40 per cent, in Southern Asia and the Middle East about 25 per cent, and it is at its lowest in sub-Saharan Africa where less than 10 per cent of married women are estimated to be using contraception.

However, even in Western Europe attitudes to and actual practice of contraception are very variable. A recent survey of contraceptive use by young Europeans reported that:

a) in the majority of countries girls' use of contraceptives at first intercourse is lower than boys';

b) even in those countries with a long tradition of sex education and high contraceptive use, a large proportion of young people use no contraceptive at first intercourse;

c) the younger the age the less prevalent is contraceptive use at first intercourse;

d) the incidence of unplanned pregnancy increases with the casualness of the relationship;

e) contraceptive practice is less frequent in rural compared with urban environments;

f) the degree to which a country is urbanised increases contraceptive usage;

g) contraceptive usage increases with age and the number of coital experiences.

Opposition to contraception in Europe is based on views similar, if more sophisticatedly expressed, to those heard on the shores of Lake Victoria. Contraception is detrimental to health, say its critics, is immoral, contrary to religious teaching, deprives sexuality of its natural spontaneity, is ineffective, encourages promiscuity and fosters venereal disease. In Poland, particularly in rural areas, couples appear to rely in the

> The Government of Portugal provided a striking example of a
> first major initiative to create family-planning services, which
> began in 1976 when there had been approximately 19,000
> consultations in existing services. In 1982, the number
> approached 150,000. From 1975 to 1979, the child mortality rate
> declined by 12·9 per 1000, the maternal mortality rate declined
> by 12 per 1000 and the proportion of unassisted births declined
> from 30 per cent in 1970 to 10 per cent in 1979. In 1984, laws
> on maternity protection, sexual education and family planning,
> and abortion were passed. It is interesting to note that
> the main factors listed as contributing to the success of
> the programme were the availability of information from
> the Commission on the Status of Women, health education
> departments' efforts, through the media, to increase the
> awareness of women and their progressive participation in
> socio-economic life and the higher educational levels of the
> younger generations.[2]
>
> United Nations Report, Nairobi, 1985

main on the so-called rhythm method or on coitus interruptus, while in Spain, Italy and most Eastern European countries (Hungary being the notable exception), withdrawal, the rhythm method and abstinence are reportedly the most prevalent forms of contraception used.

Women who do not want to have babies will go to virtually any lengths to prevent it. Induced abortion is widespread even where it is illegal. Somewhere between 30 and 50 million abortions are believed to be performed worldwide every year. In many countries, developed and developing, it is illegal while in other countries, most notably China, Japan, Korea, Cuba and Bulgaria, it is an important and socially accepted method of regulating family size. In Europe, a growing number of young women have induced abortions, presumably a consequence of increasingly early and widespread premarital intercourse without contraceptive protection.

In Hungary, official policy on abortion has undergone rapid revision over the years. During the early post-war years, the deliberate interruption of a pregnancy had to be carried out only for firm medical reasons; as a result the number of legal abortions performed was between 2000 and 3000 per year. At the same time, however, an estimated 100,000 to 150,000 illegal abortions per year were believed to be performed. In 1954, the law was changed. Abortion was to be permitted on social grounds up to the twelfth week of pregnancy; the social grounds included the age of the mother and stressful socio-economic circumstances such as overcrowding. As a direct result, abortion virtually on demand was permitted and the abortion rate rapidly climbed to a peak of 192,000 in 1970 or 127 abortions for every 100 live births. Any pregnant woman could request an abortion and no one would examine her psychological or social justifications, let alone her medical ones. With the increase in availability of contraceptive methods in the 1970s, the abortion rate began to fall but it was still 170,000 in 1978 when, concerned by the rate and the effect on Hungary's population structure, the government imposed new restrictions. The rate continued to fall but quickly levelled out at its present rate of some 80,000 per year.

It has been estimated that about 25 per cent of legal abortions in Hungary are carried out on women who are unmarried, a further 33 per cent take place because the woman has reached her preferred quota of live children (at least two), 16 per cent involve medical reasons, 16 per cent are performed on grounds of housing difficulties, and the remainder are for other, largely social, reasons. To obtain an abortion on grounds other than medical ones, a woman has to put her case before an abortion review committee. The committee, made up of a doctor, a health visitor and a representative of the social services, hears the arguments and then makes the decision. An appeals committee exists with a similar composition plus a representative of the trade unions and a local council official, to which dissatisfied applicants can make representation.

Italy, like Hungary, has a low birth rate. It also has one of the lowest take-up rates of contraception and one of the highest rates of abortion. There are some 1500 State family-planning clinics in the country and an equivalent number of private ones but in general Italian women remain somewhat suspicious of contraception. Dr Ines Pelaggi is a gynaecologist who works in the hospital at Catanzaro in southern Italy. Her major problems are trying to convince Italian women of the relative safety of modern contraceptive methods and the importance of trying to avoid abortion. Younger and younger women are coming to the hospital clinic for advice and they come from all social back-

> *The work of the committee reflects social control. It is designed to*
> *carry out tasks connected with population policies in Hungary.*
> *The committee helps to decide for the individual, for the woman,*
> *a question, that is equally very important for herself and for*
> *the society, the question of when the child should be born. The*
> *committee helps in these matters. It has been known to happen,*
> *and I speak from experience, that the woman realised after*
> *our conversation that the child would be a desired new member*
> *of the family and though at first she thought that the time was*
> *not right, when we discussed all the problems together, she*
> *decided to keep the baby. That is why the work of the committee*
> *is so important.*
>
> *Woman member of a Hungarian*
> *abortion appeals committee*

grounds and levels of education. She laments the fact that there is only one family-planning advice centre serving the 120,000 people of Catanzaro and its environs and the fact that her clinic is the only one whose services are free. The lack of contraception and the steady fall in the birth rate are easily explained by the high abortion rate – surprising in a country immensely influenced by the Roman Catholic Church.

Dr Pelaggi explains that the life histories of fifty-year-old women in the town commonly reveal a family size of some five children and two 'secret' abortions. Abortion, legal and illegal, has long been a method whereby women have regulated their family size. The women in Dr Pelaggi's clinic who had had abortions (and some had had up to four) spoke fatalistically about the subject. They regretted it but saw it as part of a woman's lot. Married and unmarried, young and old, they regarded abortion as a fact of their lives.

The Italian Abortion Act of 1978 permits abortion up to the twelfth week of pregnancy on medical and socio-economic grounds. The Act applies to minors under sixteen, provided consent is obtained from parents or a judge. Abortions may be performed in hospitals and authorised private clinics. The law is more fully implemented in the north and central regions of Italy than in the south, where facilities and services are lacking in both the public and the private sectors. As a consequence, illegal abortions, while less frequently undertaken, are still a feature.

Across the world in Japan, within a very different culture, a similar picture is seen. The country has one of the highest abortion rates in the world and the majority of the women involved, as in Italy, are married. Abortion represents a significant part of the income of obstetricians and gynaecologists. As some indication of the extent of income involved, an investigation of 723 obstetrical and gynaecological facilities conducted by the Japanese government's tax bureau in 1973 unearthed over £6 million in untaxed income, practically all of which was from unreported abortions.

By the time they are forty years old, two in every three Japanese women have had an abortion. The oral contraceptive pill can be obtained but can be prescribed only to regulate the menstrual cycle; side-effects have led to it not being approved for contraceptive purposes. Only the old, high-dose brands are available; they are expensive and less than 5 per cent of women use them to prevent pregnancy.

There is much evidence in Japan, as throughout the world, that contraception tends to be left to women. A direct question on the subject to Japanese spouses of either sex, according to Samuel Coleman,[3] would provide little information 'because husbands and wives are loath to reveal any signs of discord in their marriages'. However, the main method of male contraception, the condom, has required special marketing techniques to overcome embarrassment and considerable resistance to its use.

Marketing innovations aimed at lessening embarrassment at drugstores and shops retailing condoms include locating condom displays next to the cash register, pre-wrapping boxes in nondescript paper, and pricing in denominations that make speedy and inconspicuous transactions possible. The most effective sales strategy, however, has been the door-to-door commercial distribution. Samuel Coleman records how the first of the home sales companies was begun by a man whose brother ran a pharmacy; struck by the discomfort of customers purchasing condoms, he was inspired with the idea of selling them in the privacy of the customer's home.

But the task of obtaining condoms typically devolves on wives, and, emphasising the extent to which contraception is a woman's affair, even the door-to-door salespersons are women

– known in the trade as 'skin ladies'. Female customers buy in large supply and the 'skin lady' is an influential authority figure for the young wife.

It is in Japan that one encounters, very explicitly, one of the most powerful motives for having children – the fact that motherhood confers a sense of legitimacy upon female sexuality. For Japanese women, child-bearing is, as we have seen in Chapter 3, the touchstone of feminine sexual identity. Samuel Coleman, writing in the prestigious women's magazine *Fujin Koron*, summed up the prevailing sentiment,

> How does a woman change when she marries and gives birth to children? . . . This statement of the problem itself is fundamentally mistaken. It is not how a woman changes, but the fact that through marriage and childbirth she becomes a woman for the first time.[4]

Given that fact, how do Japanese women cope with the experience of abortion? The prevalence might suggest a somewhat cavalier attitude towards disposing of unwanted foetuses. In central Tokyo there is a shrine to the child Buddha, Mizuko Jizo, which is filled with tiny statues of the sacred child which have been placed there by women who have had abortions or still births or whose babies died in infancy. A survey of Japanese women's attitudes to abortion by Samuel Coleman suggested that the expression of regret, 'if it had lived', appears to be a common feeling experienced by older women. When younger, he suggests, they may have been faced with social and economic difficulties which made the pregnancy untenable. With subsequent affluence, the memories of their reasons for not proceeding with the pregnancy may well fade. In addition, both partners may nurture a particular feeling of loss if they wanted a child of one sex but have children of the other sex.

Dr Ines Pelaggi in Catanzaro distinguishes between the attitudes of younger and older women to abortion. Women who have never had children, she suggests, experience abortion in 'a slightly superficial way', that is to say they face it with less fear and fewer scruples. Women who have already had children find abortion more distressing. Caterina, married and with two children, then had an abortion which, seven years later, she still feels was the correct choice. But she continues to feel guilt, particularly when she thinks of the age her aborted child would be now. Her mother, who had eleven children, provides strong emotional support. Italian women who have had terminations cope in various ways, mostly successfully Dr Pelaggi says, with the fact that they are in conflict with their Church.

In general, moderate to severe feelings of guilt are commonly recorded after legal and illegal abortions, according to studies undertaken in Scandinavia, the US and the UK. Typically, such feelings are shortlived. However, two British researchers, Channi Kumar and Kay Robson, have found evidence suggesting that feelings of guilt and grief can persist and in some instances remain relatively quiescent until they are 're-awakened' by a subsequent pregnancy.

Self-imposed limits on fertility, through the use of contraception and abortion, are increasingly seen to hold the key to greater freedom of choice for people living in the developing and the developed countries. Yet, one of the consequences of this development is that children are at risk of being de-humanised, seen as mere products of conception, and, like other products in an increasingly commercialised world, valued on economic grounds. One of the choices increasingly circumscribed has been that of larger families. In the view of American sociologist, Barbara Katz Rothman, 'North American society is geared to small families, if indeed to any children at all. Without the provision of good medical care, day care, decent housing and schooling, children are a luxury item, fine if you can afford them.'[5]

How much choice do couples really have in opting to have children or not? Any analysis of a woman's right to have or not have a child, to have or not have an abortion, has to recognise the context in which the choice is made, the circumstances in which the woman is placed. As Rosalind Petchesky has put it,

The 'right to choose' means very little when women are powerless . . . Women make their own reproductive choices but they do not make them under conditions which they themselves create, but under social conditions and constraints which they, as mere individuals, are powerless to change.[6]

Barbara Katz Rothman is particularly struck by this illusion of choice in relation to the question of mentally-handicapped children. The introduction of amniocentesis and selective

Right Traditionally, Muslim marriages have been founded upon a contract between the groom and the bride's father. Even now the bride only signs the contract as a witness

Below The belly dance is a traditional feature of wedding celebrations in Egypt

Left *A childless woman hangs up a symbolic cradle at the Kamakshi Temple near Madras. The goddess Kamakshi is famous for answering the prayers of women who want to have children*

Below *Even Florence Malande, the local family-planning counsellor, has seven children of her own. Her husband wanted her to carry on having babies until she produced sons*

Above The recent
compulsory one-child
policy enforced by the
Chinese government
has had a remarkable
effect on slowing down
the Chinese
population growth
but its success may
prove to be China's
downfall. The new
generation of single
children are said to be
spoilt and self-centred
and not in the least bit
interested in working
for the good of the
country

Above A Kenyan man
visits his wife and
family who live in the
country. In Nairobi,
where he works during
the week, he has a
girlfriend and a child

Below This Kenyan
fishing co-operative is
run entirely by women.
Such initiatives
attempt to give women
economic
independence

The shrine to the child
Buddha, Mizuko Jizo.
The statues of the
sacred child have been
placed here by women
who have had
abortions or still births

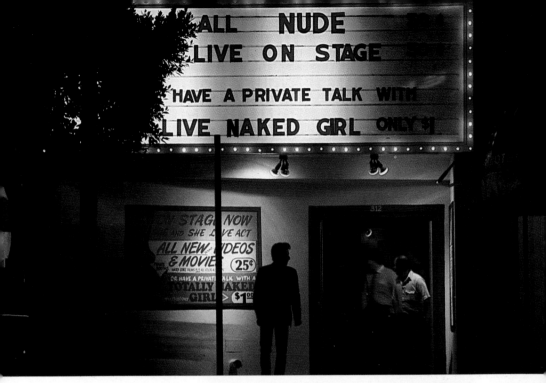

Above left *In America women can enjoy the same sort of nightlife as men*

Below left *Japanese men spend most evenings with their office colleagues at the local hostess-bar. Kisses and cuddles and risqué jokes, create an erotic atmosphere*

Above and right *Sexual titillation is easily available in California but the growing concern about sexually transmitted diseases has encouraged entertainment which does not involve physical contact. The nude girl on the end of the phone is separated from her customer by a sheet of glass*

Above Polygamous
wives from Nigeria.
The custom of dressing
wives in similar
clothing indicates the
husband's wealth and
his desire to treat the
women fairly. Most
African women
disapprove of the
custom, and the
tradition is dying out

Left A decade ago
children like this boy
labourer were valued
as workers, as the
majority of Kenyans
lived off the land. Now
Kenya has a
cash-based economy.
Children have become
expensive to raise and
they rarely contribute
to the family budget

abortion gives the impression of choice, she argues, which allows the individuals concerned to believe that they have gained control over the products of conception. But the choices are made within an 'ever-narrowing structure'. Women know that children with 'special needs' make special demands and that society as a whole is unwilling to meet these demands. After all, many societies appear unwilling to meet the demands of ordinary children.

> We live in a system in which women and children are both devalued, an anti-child, anti-woman society. It is women and children who are poor, whose needs are not being met. In this system women and children are pitted against each other competing for scarce resources. The mother finds herself becoming a resource: her own life, and specifically her own time, to be divided between herself and her children . . . The burden of child-rearing, of all child-rearing, has fallen overwhelmingly on individual mothers . . . children, all children, can be described as burdensome when their needs fall exclusively on one person.[7]

In a modern, industrialised society such as Britain, children are seen as costly. They cost more than they are financially worth in a society which increasingly values everything in cash terms. Almost all the children conceived in Britain will survive to adult life if not aborted. State pensions and the growth of life assurance reassure many of us that old age will be tolerable whether our children are around to make it so or not. There is still status to be gained from having children, and the childless, whether so by accident or choice, have to negotiate a curious, disapproving, sometimes even hostile society. Having more than the socially approved number can provoke similar disapproval.

All that remains to motivate couples to have children is the hope that children will remind us of the eternal throb of life connecting us to our earliest ancestors and will guarantee that some remnant of our genes, our blood, our presence will continue to be here on Earth long after we are but dust. And, of course, children make us happy.

Children making us happy are required to join the lengthening list of consumer durables, luxuries, experiences, baubles, bangles and beads for which a similar claim is raucously bellowed in every glossy magazine and brash television advertisement. The costly child now takes its place beside the beach villa holiday, the wrought-iron garden equipment, the cars and the furs and the hundred and one other inanimate items of the twentieth-century bazaar which promise to make us happy too. But the problem with children is that they can also make us unhappy and, unlike all the other goodies in the mail-order catalogues, the wretched things have demands and needs of their own. Daily, we are confronted with evidence that babies are not always regarded as adorable; the battering, the neglect, the starvation of children can be seen as warning signs that we may have replaced traditional, prosaic, pragmatic motives for having children with a highly romantic and idealised notion of the purpose and the promise of childbirth and child-rearing.

Such a romantic notion, if it exists, does so within a society which, as Barbara Katz Rothman pugnaciously argues, is not particularly pro-child. Indeed, a recent analysis by David Piachaud for the Study Commission on the Family[8] has shown that, compared with the net income of a childless couple, State support for families of all sizes in Britain has steadily declined in real terms between 1965 and 1981, with the rate of decline increasing in recent years. Other societies, such as Hungary and Norway, struggle to make the choice of having a child competitive with buying a new car or obtaining a house, but the task is made doubly difficult given the fact that the women who are to bear the children are themselves tempted into the job market to swell the family income to maintain the living standards of the families they already have. As we have seen, women come off badly in this conflict of roles, whether it be in developing or developed countries. That elusive free choice, much trumpeted by the birth controllers and the economists, still remains elusive while social expectations, attitudes, values and political policies, the customs and the laws which surround and constrain the decision to have a child, turn out on closer examination to be as crucial determinants as they have ever been.

5 THE LIMITS OF FIDELITY

The expectations we have of the institution of marriage in Western society in the latter half of the twentieth century are truly remarkable. The three cardinal features of the Judaeo-Christian vision of marriage – its indissolubility, its emphasis on child-bearing and fidelity – still exercise a powerful appeal. Within marriage we are encouraged to find intimacy, companionship and dependence. But the newer values of what has been termed the human potential movement which began to emerge during the 1950s and 1960s suggest that within marriage the partners are also engaged in a search to find themselves and each other; both searches are lifelong and neither is guaranteed to progress in such a way as to ensure the survival of the marriage itself. Where once marriage was seen through prosaic eyes as a public contract legitimising sexual union, embodying a permanent social relationship and prescribing certain obligations regarding family, parenthood and a place of residence, now it is viewed through more rosy spectacles and the stated goals include personal growth, sexual fulfilment and mutual emotional satisfaction.

Such expectations, of course, quickly proved to be contradictory. What if my personal fulfilment requires me to experience that tempting extramarital relationship whereas my spouse's fulfilment requires that I remain faithful? What if, despite my most vigorous efforts, I experience profound feelings of jealousy when confronted by the fact that my spouse, in her search for sexual fulfilment, finds herself in another bed than ours? The advocates of the so-called sexual revolution bit on this particular bullet and concluded that the bonds of fidelity and the impulses of jealousy were nothing more than unresolved symptoms of childish immaturity and infantile possessiveness. One of the gurus of the revolution, Dr Alex Comfort, in More Joy of Sex,[1] even compared sexual jealousy to the behaviour of 'a

backward five-year-old who sees another child with his tri-
cycle'.

Some years ago I travelled around California exploring the
growth of the cults and psychotherapies for which that part of
America had become famous. No such trip could have been
complete without a visit to Esalen, the self-styled university of
experience between San Francisco and Los Angeles. People
come to Esalen from all over America, to savour the mineral
baths and the nutritious food, the balmy weather and the
beautiful scenery, and to be massaged, counselled, analysed
and reborn. On the wall of my log cabin was a poster containing
an exhortation from Fritz Perls, one of the leading advocates of
the human potential movement,

> I do my thing, you do your thing. I am not in this world to live up to your
> expectations and you are not in this world to live up to mine! You are you
> and I am I, and if by chance we meet, it's beautiful, if not, it can't be helped.

This unequivocal proclamation constitutes an endorsement of
one of the central tenets of American life, namely the notion of
the autonomous individual as the ultimate bearer of responsibility for his or her psyche. Indeed, two psychiatrists, Wen-shing
Tseng and J. F. McDermott, commenting on psychotherapy in
the United States as seen through Eastern eyes, observed that
within American society, in which self-sufficiency and responsibility are highly idealised, it is often difficult to find opportunities for the satisfaction of dependency needs (jargon for needing
someone else to love and depend upon), save in the socially
approved relationship with a personal psychotherapist! And
within many of those psychotherapeutic relationships, individuals are encouraged to explore their so-called dependency needs
in order to be freed of them. Dependence, need, possessiveness –
these are childish vices to be rooted out, relentlessly analysed
and then despatched. The goal is adulthood – and adulthood, as
outlined in the assertive, self-reliant, self-fulfilling new Athens
that is California, means putting yourself first.

For this reason, California is the obvious place to go if you are
intrigued by the notion of a contemporary society in which
sexual fidelity is explicitly put aside and yet marriage as a
recognisable institution still remains. California is, after all, a
place where every effort is made to satisfy every known sexual

need and aberration. It epitomises Tom Wolfe's 'Me Decade' with its open invitation to any one of us that since we only have one life let us be Brigitte Bardot or Paul Getty, sexually experienced and personally fulfilled.

Ten years on from Tom Wolfe's 'Me Decade', *Lovelaw* went to see what had happened to those high hopes of sexual freedom and liberation. Had jealousy, supposedly the dragon which slays love under the pretence of keeping it alive, itself been slain? Or is there something in that German proverb which says that where there is no jealousy there is no love?

Jenny and Ed Harwood were married fifteen years ago right in the middle of this exciting time for human potential and personal growth. Some five years into the marriage, Ed felt the need to experience extramarital sex. He confessed to Jenny his curiosity about what a purely sexual relationship with another woman would be like. Jenny knew the importance of personal freedom and sensed that her possessive and jealous feelings reflected childish impulses not 'worked through'. Ed, whose work took him away from home at regular intervals, had a few affairs and Jenny coped – but with difficulty. She still felt threatened in a way she found difficult to put into words. When, however, one of Ed's affairs looked like becoming more than just a sexual fling, words came,

> I was intensely jealous and threatened. I harassed him on the phone. I called him and when he came back home I really confronted him with the issue. All of a sudden it looked a lot bigger than just fooling around. It felt, you know, a natural physical feeling at that moment, it felt scary. I felt I could not stand it, 'this is too scary for me'; I was scared that he would want to be with that other person and not come back . . .

Of course Ed had given Jenny her freedom to experiment extramaritally but, for reasons not altogether clear, Jenny felt the need to do so far less than did her husband. As far as Ed was concerned, sexual relations *per se* were not particularly threatening. But he too felt somewhat less secure about a relationship outside marriage which would consume energy and dilute investment in the marital relationship. Indeed, the one time Ed felt threatened was when Jenny became active in some psychotherapy workshops and had become emotionally very involved. 'I felt that I was actually losing Jenny and that her attention was not going to be focused on our relationship.'

Of course Jenny and Ed may just not have sufficiently worked through the remnants of childhood dependency and emotional immaturity. Jenny even admitted that her own self-esteem was bound up with the idea of Ed being faithful, while Ed confessed to a fear of 'losing' his wife, indicating by his choice of words a deplorable possessiveness! Be that as it may, the pair of them, older, perhaps wiser and with three small children, have turned away from extramarital exploration and have settled for a faithful relationship. Ed stresses the prosaic reason that a large family demands so much emotional commitment that there is little left for expenditure outside his marriage. Jenny acknowledges that her view of herself is bound up with her husband's view of her. 'Be jealous,' she exhorts him, only half-joking.

Dr Danny Slomoff and his wife Lucy Mercer have also rejected the completely open marriage but they believe that sexual infidelity is none the less inevitable and should be acknowledged rather than kept hidden. Their answer is a series of careful rules designed to protect each other and to preserve their marriage. When either of them travels, and again their jobs take them away quite regularly, sexual affairs are permitted. But there is an absolute ban on affairs with anyone in their home town. There is also an absolute right to put a veto on any relationship. As Danny Slomoff explains it,

> If Lucy closes it down [that is, insists that he stop being involved with someone], I can never discuss it or disagree. I must agree to her wishes and the same applies to her. The assumption is that she is closing it down because she is feeling unsure of herself or, if I am closing a relationship of hers down, I am feeling unsure of myself. If either of us continued to have it open, we would just be festering a wound rather than maintaining a closer relationship.

Lucy admits that her husband takes advantage of their arrangement to have affairs more frequently than she does. She also admits to jealousy although she struggles to keep it under control. She feels it is much easier for her husband to get in and out of affairs and still remain committed to their marriage. She wonders whether this difference between them has something to do with the possibility that women find it more difficult than men to separate sexual activity from love and the development of a relationship.

Danny insists that he does not become jealous because sex is really not that important. But if it is not that important cannot the extramarital variety be set aside, sacrificed for the sake of marital commitment? Would it be so hard to forgo extramarital experience? Danny's reply is revealing,

> When I meet somebody, could be a friend who I have known for a long time, part of our friendship, part of the response that both of us are having, the evening out, the time together, part of that friendship can include sexuality. It doesn't have to but at times it can. There is almost like this strange line that people draw when they meet one another whereby they say, 'OK, I really enjoy you, I like you very much,' and then you hug and there are some sparks that fly between you and you say, 'Oh gosh, I can't do anything; I can't respond; I'm not allowed.' And you cut yourself off at that point. Or, then again, some people follow it up to a certain point – they admit that they can't have intercourse but they can kiss, they can take off their clothes and be passionate but intercourse is where fidelity stops and starts . . .

Danny Slomoff believes that 'this strange line' which people draw is an unnecessary limit, an interference in the normal, healthy expression of feelings between friends or acquaintances. Only if the full expression of sexual feelings distresses one or other of the marital partners is it taboo. They both accept that each of them can be distressed and their feelings are paramount. Yet again, however, there seems regret, particularly on Danny's part, that they continue to be confronted by the persistence of jealousy.

Philip Miller and his wife Gypsy Koch are convinced that they have slain the dragon. Philip, a self-employed craftsman carpenter, and Gypsy, a midwife, have four children and are expecting a fifth. They live an ordinary domestic life and look for all the world the very epitome of a settled, suburban couple. They are deeply committed to each other and to the marriage but both regularly have sexual relations with other people. Again there are rules but in this instance they seem to amount to little more than sorting out who is responsible for organising the baby-sitter when both of them go 'swinging'. For their usual outlet for sexual excitement is a joint visit to a local 'swing' party where couples exchange partners.

Like many who emigrated to California, Philip comes from the mid-West and was attracted to the west coast because it seemed an enlightened place compared with his native Indiana. He retained 'old-fashioned' notions of marriage, which included not going to bed with anyone other than one's wife, until he met and married Gypsy. It was she who introduced him to the swinging scene. When they were first married, they each had their own room and telephone and made their own dates, having asked for 'permission' in advance. Philip went along with this although to begin with he felt odd and uncomfortable. Gradually, however, he overcame the last vestiges of jealousy, that emotion which according to both of them arises out of personal insecurity. They insist they are emotionally faithful. Sex with others is recreation, pleasurable, fun, no big deal. They are honest, upfront and frank. When they decide on a pregnancy, they refrain from extramarital sex. And, given the concern about contracting AIDS, they are careful with whom they sleep. As for morality – the golden rule is not 'Thou shalt not commit adultery' but 'Thou shalt not hurt anyone knowingly or unknowingly.' And what of the risk that one or other of them will fall in love with a 'swinging' partner? 'You don't need to go to a swing party,' observes Gypsy, 'to fall into one relationship and out of another.'

The key characteristics of the sexually liberated society – the availability and effectiveness of modern contraception, the sexual equality of the two sexes, the opportunities provided by mobility and leisure and the adoption of a blatantly utilitarian and pleasure-oriented philosophy of life – all conspire to produce a scenario which would give the Pope a nightmare. Such behaviour is conventionally seen as destructive to normal family life. But infidelity is one of the main destroyers and Philip and Gypsy insist they have it tamed. Sex, when not employed in the service of procreation, has become purely recreational – just like earlier Popes said it would!

Another society which has a recreational view of sexual activity is Japan but here there is in its operation something of a double standard. In general, it is the men who have the sexual fun. The conventional wisdom in the West concerning Japan is that the Japanese acknowledge the legitimacy of sex as a human desire but keep it firmly in its place. Sex is circumscribed by social controls and duties, in contrast with the West where it is overloaded with guilt and repression. There is, at the heart of all of this, the implication that compared with Western men the Japanese male is less bothered by sexual matters.

Bothered he may not be but preoccupied he certainly is. Every day on Japanese underground trains can be seen numerous men openly reading paperback books and magazines illustrated with crudely drawn cartoons of quite astonishing explicitness. Romances of a Mills & Boon quality are highlighted by pictures of coupling men and women and drawings more appropriately found in gynaecological texts. Japanese cinema, too, offers the viewer a diet of pornographic films.

The foreign visitor is tempted to believe that this all testifies to the sophisticated and guilt-free attitudes towards sex which mark Japan. But, as Samuel Coleman has pointed out, such a view misses the important point that the context of such sexual explicitness is completely male-oriented,

> The word used for pleasure in 'sex for pleasure', *kairaku*, has a definitely pejorative association with hedonism, as well as nuances of selfishness, and submission to basic urges. This negative cast, subsumed in the 'sex-as-pleasure' orientation, fits well with the attitude that the man dedicated to his work pays less attention to such matters since they are essentially frivolous. The combination of sexual titillation in men's entertainment with penalties for an open interest in sex has created – quite predictably – a hypocritical bent, which Japanese themselves have labelled with the slang expression 'closet lecher' (*muttsuri sukebei*).[2]

Recreational sex, sex as an escape from hard work, sex as frivolity and titillation – such a sexuality is deemed intolerable in Japanese society where a more full-blooded, a more rounded form might elbow out the more important values of duty, discipline and work. Men can quite openly and without embarrassment read graphically illustrated porn in public, whereas there are still quite strong taboos on the public expression of affection. Young people, it is true, are increasingly to be seen walking arm-in-arm. But the older the Japanese the greater the tendency to insist that matters of love and affection be kept private.

And such a compartmentalisation of sexuality as a release, an escape, an entertainment colours Japanese attitudes towards infidelity. While the great majority of Japanese men sternly disapprove of female extramarital activity, they themselves spend evenings after work in hostess-bars and take all-male group holidays in Korea and Thailand for 'rest and recreation'. It is security that the Japanese husband promises to give his wife, not fidelity. And the Japanese wife accepts it as a fact of male life. Recreational sex she can tolerate but, rather like Jenny Harwood and Lucy Mercer in California, it is the extramarital affair which might involve significant emotional intimacy which threatens her and causes real anxiety.

In Kyoto, suburban family man and industrial executive Mr Himeno Yoshida is interviewed by *Lovelaw* concerning the pragmatic split between marriage and sexuality. His extramarital liaisons afford him no guilt unless they lead him to cancel some family arrangement. His wife is tolerant of his regular trips to Korea for she understands that the main purpose of such trips is 'playing at love and purely physical things'. She knows that any women involved in such trips are paid for. 'It is quite another thing,' he points out, 'when I have affairs with women colleagues in the office and with women I meet through business.' Such women can constitute a very real danger to the Yoshida marriage. Mr Yoshida admits that he enjoys brief affairs with educated and cultured women and finds with them excitement and intellectual stimulation not always available in his marriage. But, in general, he is careful to restrict his extramarital activities to sex-for-pleasure encounters in the hostess-bars he frequents with business colleagues after work. And what of his wife, Noriko? She confesses that she knows that her husband sleeps with other women. She tolerates it because it is the norm and because she has no real choice. But she does not like it. She has three children, aged nine, seven and five, and this family is utterly dependent on Mr Yoshida for economic and social survival. When asked why Japanese men so openly seek sexual pleasure outside the home, she replies,

> As everyone knows, there are so many diversions to attract men outside the home, such as bars and pretty unfettered hostesses. At home, he can behave as a family man but it is only when he is outside the home that the trouble arises after business hours and probably in the company of business acquaintances. Another aspect of the question is the ease with which the man can suddenly decide to seek enjoyment outside which is not the same for the woman. She must consider many household and family tasks before she decides to go out. But I must emphasise again: men find themselves surrounded by attractive women who are completely unfettered and ready to lure them into false circumstances.

It looks like a re-emergence of that old double standard again. Noriko could, technically, avail herself of extramarital affairs – her husband chivalrously concedes to the *Lovelaw* interviewer that she is a free agent – but in fact her domestic responsibilities make such a thing a matter of fantasy only. Meanwhile her husband, along with many a Japanese man, accepts a situation which effectively institutionalises that well-known split whereby women are stereotyped as either domestic matron or seductive whore.

The *Mama-san*, manageress and guiding spirit of one of Mr Yoshida's favourite hostess-bars, explains the role of the hostess-bar and the girls that are there to satisfy the male customers' diverse needs. She and her girls provide a willing and expert ear for harassed executives, businessmen, industrialists and skilled workers, enabling them to air their feelings and articulate their worries. Japanese preoccupations about 'losing face' make it difficult for the average man to take home to his wife and family his worries, difficulties and dissatisfactions relating to his work.

The other main reason for the popularity of such settings is sexual recreation. But, once again, there is an odd aura of childhood and a mummy making things better and reassuring the worn-out and battered male refugee from the Japanese industrial scene that he is doing very well and is really a splendid little fellow. Her customers address the *Mama-san* sometimes as *oba-chan* (auntie) and even as *ola-chan* (mummy). Many of the men come to play baby son to the *Mama-san* or one of her girls. The *Mama-san* takes a positively maternal view of her men's needs. Men need a variety of different things from women, she observes, and it is perfectly reasonable that they should seek domesticity, support and affection from their wives while also seeking intellectual stimulation from a female work colleague and sexual satisfaction from a hostess-girl.

And *Mama-san* plays the role of sex-counsellor too. In Japan, you don't have to ring up a radio sex-expert or write to an agony columnist for advice about sexual positions or the efficacy of aphrodisiacs. You can just drop into *Mama-san*'s bar and sort out the theory, and the practice too, with your favourite hostess.

But much of what goes on in such bars does not involve sex. Instead, there is much singing of songs, drinking and childish joking with the girls who mother and mollify their somewhat unruly men. There is much to suggest a mother-son quality to these interactions. Every Japanese male is emotionally very involved with his mother, while the Japanese woman, on becoming a mother, ceases to be a sexual person for the most part and invests considerable emotional feeling in her children and, in particular, in her sons.

Keiko Higuchi, a Japanese writer and commentator on women's issues, points out that for Japanese women the children form the social focal point of their lives,

> The mother prefers her children (usually two in number) not to become independent, for their presence is her only source of pleasure. Children today do not bother to say goodbye to their mother before leaving for school. It is the mother who checks the contents of the child's school satchel, closes it and puts it on the child's back. As she does so she anticipates the child's farewell, saying, 'See you later. Take care now.' The child need only nod graciously. The mother arranges everything for the children. All they have to do is decide whether to nod or shake their heads like young lords.[3]

But Japan is a society in transition. If traditional Japanese values permit the male to be unfaithful while ensuring that his wife is restricted to the home, the trends towards smaller families, increasing employment for women outside the home and a growing female assertiveness must surely exercise an effect on the hostess-bar culture and the sex-as-recreation philosophy. But in which direction? Will Japan imitate California so that Noriko, like Gypsy, can enjoy the sexual freedom currently available to her husband? Or will it move in the direction taken by another country in transition, Egypt?

Egypt, as mentioned before, is in the midst of a flowering of Islamic fundamentalism. The freedom which many middle-class Egyptians enjoyed and which permitted them to experiment sexually over the past decade shows signs of being constrained. Yes, there is infidelity in the Egyptian middle classes, concedes psychologist Dr Muhammad Sha'alan, but much less of it than a few years ago and it is strongly disapproved of. Extramarital activity is not helped by the fact that, in Cairo at any rate, people live in each other's pockets in one of the world's most densely populated cities. Private extramarital liaisons and assignations are, as a result, extraordinarily difficult to arrange. The Egyptian woman having an affair behaves a little like Madame Bovary but, whereas Flaubert's heroine conducted her extramarital adventure in a closed carriage, Egyptian adultery is often even less comfortable. As Dr Sha'alan describes it,

> Most people are eyeball to eyeball, seeing each other as if they are in a fishbowl. A lot of rumours can spread, a reputation can be ruined. So people are very careful about having affairs. And if they do it, it has got to be secret. Generally they would either borrow an apartment or hire a room in a hotel which is again very difficult. But young people have inventive means like hiding in a car and covering it with a piece of cloth.

But there is another very good reason why Egyptians think twice before entering upon an adulterous relationship. It is, quite simply, against the law – the Islamic law *and* the Egyptian civil law, which is based upon the Napoleonic Code introduced by the French in the early nineteenth century. Whereas Islamic law punishes both sexes equally, Egyptian law adopts a double standard. The Egyptian adulterous woman, wherever she commits the offence, is punished; the Egyptian male is punished only if his adultery takes place in the matrimonial home. Because the man's work is outside the home this area is seen to be his kingdom where he may do as he will. But Muslims consider the matrimonial home to be the woman's sphere of influence and so a husband committing adultery in the home is committing an assault on his wife's kingdom. The law lays down up to three years' imprisonment for the offence but, as senior judge Dr Gamal Mahmoud explains, society's view of the adulterous man and the adulterous woman is not a balanced one,

> There is a great difference in the way that society looks upon the man and the woman. It is not as hard on the man as it is on the woman. The woman who commits this crime stays for the rest of her life feeling ashamed and the people always look at her with disrespect. There is social discrimination in this matter.

In actual fact, cases of adulterous conduct come to the courts rarely. A woman charging her husband with adultery can end up in a position akin to the woman who has been raped, blamed by society for the crime of which she has been the victim. Egyptian law demands that the accused be caught in the act or that there be incriminating letters and so on, while Islamic law is even more stringent and requires four witnesses at the time the crime is committed.

None the less, insists the judge, and Dr Sha'alan agrees with him, adultery in Egypt is nothing like as common an occurrence as it is in the permissive West. Egyptian society looks upon the man or the woman who commits adultery as a person with no religious belief, a person who is led by lust and who cannot be trusted. The enormous social disapproval, the general lack of opportunity, and the separation of many women from opportunities for infidelity together contribute to a situation where extramarital activity is more the exception than the rule. Dr Sha'alan concedes that a more permissive attitude towards fidelity and infidelity may exist amongst what he terms 'the lower or poorer classes' but, in general, the Egyptian middle class maintains a puritanical and conservative attitude to the subject.

Another factor which may well act as a disincentive to infidelity is polygamy. Polygamous marriage, like circumcision, is gradually becoming outmoded in cities such as Cairo and Alexandria yet the fact remains that by law an Egyptian male is entitled to have up to four wives at any one time. Because a man may be expected to offer marriage to any woman he sexually solicits, men may be very cautious when tempted to engage in extramarital activities. In Dr Sha'alan's words, 'The fact that you're allowed to marry another woman, in addition to your wife, makes you hesitate about having an affair with another woman.'

To many Egyptians, Western morality signifies complete freedom and complete indifference to moral considerations. Dr Sha'alan's work took him for a number of years to California, a state which seemed to him at the time to be like Paradise, where, in his words, 'Adam and Eve had no clothes, there was no marriage, and no ceremonies and just free choice.' During his 'American' phase he went through a succession of marriages. It was a sort of serial polygamy unlike the marital career of his own father, a rural farmer who was married nine times although he never had more than his legal entitlement of four wives at any one time. Having experienced what, in retrospect, he sees as a repressive and restrictive youth in rural Egypt and an experimental and open phase in swinging California, Dr Sha'alan has now settled for a marriage in which freedom is the ability to accept limits, to be able to say to one's spouse, 'I freely give you the right to hold me and to restrict my freedom.' Instead of wasting time and energy seeking sexual fulfilment and intellectual satisfaction in three or four affairs, he concentrates on finding in his marriage the qualities of affection, friendship, commitment and fidelity – 'everything we are looking for in another person'.

In Kenya, attitudes towards infidelity are also affected by the age-old tradition of polygamous relationships. In the offices of a Nairobi newspaper, *Lovelaw* filmed the editing and printing of an article entitled 'Faithful Husbands – Do They Exist?' The author, Kenyan journalist David Maillu, argues that fidelity for men is not part of the African tradition and is not considered natural. He quotes the African proverb – 'If you want to tie a man down, marry him many wives' – to explain the part played by traditional polygamous arrangements in discouraging infidelity. If a man has five wives, he explains, and engages in sexual relations with each of them he is not regarded as unfaithful; if, however, he were to have an extramarital relationship with a sixth woman then this would constitute infidelity and would warrant severe punishment which could include social ostracism. In contrast to the man who moves from one woman to another with no legal ties, the polygamous man is required to take full financial responsibility for his wives and, as David Maillu points out, this inevitably means that polygamy has tended to be the preferred practice of the better-off and hence commands high status. As the Kenyan male is judged by the number of children he has sired so he is judged by the number of women he has married.

With urbanisation, as we saw in Chapter 1, the legal constraints and responsibilities of polygamy have broken down but the Kenyan male still tends to seek and find sexual satisfaction with a variety of women. Urbanisation has led to large numbers of young men leaving the villages and migrating to Nairobi and Mombasa where they often have to stay for lengthy periods of time before returning home. Few such men can afford to take another wife in the city yet few contemplate with equanimity life without a sexual relationship. The result is the seemingly casual sexuality and promiscuity which so distresses Dr Gatere and which leads in part at least to the dilemma and predicament of girls such as Mombie (Chapter 1).

Contrasted with that chaotic urban scenario, ritualised, traditional polygamy offers the benefits of clear-cut roles, responsibilities and a stable structure. David Maillu agrees. He is well qualified to talk about polygamy. His own father had several wives and he himself accepts the possibility that he might well take another wife if, for example, his own wife became ill or inactive in some way that might mean 'sexual death'. But in taking on another wife he would not simply discard his current wife. 'I do not see anything absolutely wrong in being a polygamist,' he argues spiritedly,

George Adero, a Kenyan civil servant, has four wives. He is seen here with Monica, his fourth wife

. . . whereas the idea of just moving from one woman to another and caring little about what happens does scare me. I'm dealing with a human being and I would prefer that if we do have an affair and by any chance we have a child then that child is not labelled a bastard. So the issue of polygamy is quite an open one.

It is estimated that some 20 per cent of men and 30 per cent of women in Kenya are to be found in polygamous marriages. There are certain obvious advantages. Fertility, for example, Kenya's greatest social problem, is 11 per cent lower in polygamous than in monogamous marriages. Polygamy is associated with long periods of post-partum abstinence for the woman (two years or more) and with living arrangements wherein the husband has his own accommodation and only visits his wives at night for sexual contact. In contrast, monogamy and the co-residential household lead to far more frequent sexual relations for the male. One of the unexpected and unwanted consequences of increased female education and the opposition of the Christian Churches to polygamy has been the increase in Kenya's fertility since it has contributed to a preference for monogamy, a speedier reinstitution of sexual activity in the post-partum woman and the abandonment of traditional contraceptive practices such as prolonged breast-feeding.

So what happens to jealousy in the polygamous marriage? Are the various wives of the polygamous Kenyan jealous of each other? George Adero is a Kenyan civil servant who has four wives. His first wife, Elizabeth, has borne him seven children. His second wife, Joyce, who is Elizabeth's younger sister, has had ten. His third wife, Mary, is a teacher in nearby Kisumu. He has recently taken a fourth wife, Monica. George is in no doubt about the advantages of polygamy – for both sexes. First, by marrying several women he keeps them from roaming Kisumu, perhaps even Nairobi. Second, he says, there is the problem that wives age and, unlike men, lose their sexual potency and drive. Ostensibly he married Joyce for this reason, although later we learn from a somewhat disgruntled Elizabeth that she was actually still quite young at the time of her sister's marriage. But the main advantage, at least for George, is that his every need is met. His wives live in separate houses grouped around his own, save for Monica who, having just arrived, shares a room in Elizabeth's house. The women take it in turns to do George's cooking, cleaning and washing but otherwise maintain physically separate existences. Their children, however, mix and play together and even share sleeping accommodation. The fact that each wife has a separate house, George explains, reduces the tendency for them to quarrel. George is very eager to make it plain that in general his wives get on well together but he does admit that Mary does not like Monica and, when pressed for a reason, grudgingly concedes that jealousy 'which is always happening' may well be the problem.

And what is there in polygamy for the women? They have the security and the fact that there is someone to take care of them and their children, though this also applies to the monogamous marriages as well. There is status too, particularly for the first wife. But the main reason why Kenyan women tolerate polygamy seems to be that they have no real choice. Mary, for example, George's reluctant and seemingly difficult third wife, has little say in what happens given that George has paid a substantial dowry or bride-price for her services. He sees her as a good investment for she is a teacher with an established salary and in this country education and those providing it are genuinely valued. Unless Mary were to repay the bride-price she remains his wife and under his authority.

George strives hard to reduce jealousy, particularly sexual jealousy amongst his wives, by scrupulously arranging to spend equal time with them. It is not a nightly rota, he is quick to point out. Flitting from house to house in a series of one-night stands might distress his daughters, he observes with an unexpected primness. Instead, he tends to spend a week at a time with one or other of the wives. However, were he to linger with one wife longer than a week then jealousy might well become intense.

Elizabeth is not sure about the advantages of polygamy but does not regard sexual jealousy as the main shortcoming. She did, it is true, take his decision to marry her younger sister badly and for a while took to heavy drinking. Gradually, Joyce soothed her feelings and for a fairly lengthy period of time during which Joyce delayed having children there were just the two wives. George's marriage to Mary was not welcome, the third wife being seen by Elizabeth and Joyce as a troublesome woman. Mary apart, the remaining three wives get on reasonably well but there are clearly areas of friction. Initially, the wives shared the cooking and shopping, but differences of opinion over the proper foods for children and the amounts of money to be spent on food led to Elizabeth cooking for her own children. There is constant anxiety lest one wife and her children fail to get their just share of the family earnings and this is a much more troublesome area than the issue of sexual jealousy.

Elizabeth, in general, is resigned to her situation, thanks God for her healthy children and comforts herself that she is fulfilling her social and religious duties. George's second wife, Joyce, is more enthusiastic about polygamy but his fourth wife, Monica, is far less sanguine. She married George because she was in dire financial straits. She already had three children but their father would not agree to marry her or support her financially. There was no other young man who would marry her either. George, a man old enough to be her father, offered her help and she was in no position to refuse. She admits that in time she has come to love him and is grateful that he takes care of her and her children. She gets on well with his other wives, save for Mary, but she would prefer to have a husband to herself.

So too, it appears, would absent third wife Mary. She resents the other wives and wants George for herself. The polygamous arrangement does not meet women's needs to anything like the extent to which it meets those of men. Monica puts the issue squarely,

It is the conditions which bring about polygamous marriages. Maybe it is because so many of us Africans don't know how to prevent pregnancy. And that is the whole trouble; it is pregnancy that brings all these things. Because you get pregnant you are not loved in your own home by your parents. You decide to go away, you decide to roam, you decide to work in a bar. And then maybe the people who go in that bar treat you so badly that you decide to marry any man without knowing the type of man you are marrying. Then you may divorce the man. So, in the end, this leads us to marry this old man with so many wives. But it is not because we like it. It is because we can do nothing else.

George defends with gusto his decision to marry four wives. He married Joyce when his work took him to Nairobi and he wanted a wife to come with him and look after his needs while

Elizabeth stayed behind and cared for his farm and children. He chose Mary because she brought with her an income and he chose his fourth wife, Monica, because he genuinely felt sorry for her. But, in the final analysis, George's polygamy is not a business venture. Rather he acquires wives as Western men collect vintage cars or club memberships – because it brings him social status. Indeed, there are financial considerations which deter men from polygamy: after all, there are a large number of children to be fed, clothed and put through school. But a Kenyan male with four wives and over twenty children wields a fair amount of social influence. It is only money that prevents him from marrying more frequently. As for troubles between the wives – those quarrels over food, sexual jealousy and money, how does George cope?

> My wives bring the problem to me. If there is one who thinks that perhaps one of the others has been mistaken about her then they come to me and we sort it out. I tell them I don't like noise or jealousy or shouting at home. I tell them I would like them to leave otherwise. And if they really are all the husband's then they will follow him because if they don't follow him, if there is a wife who is stubborn then she will have to face the punishment. Because we are allowed to cane. You can cane or you can tell her to go away.

Within the polygamous marriage, the man is boss. The wife who is unable to get on with her husband or with one or more of his other wives can either buckle down or leave. In reality, she often has little choice. To leave without her children would be agony to the average Kenyan woman. To leave with them would be social suicide. Yet here again things are changing. There are powerful voices being raised against polygamy. The Church, particularly the Roman Catholic Church, has long ignored the advantages of security of marriage for most women which polygamy offers, the fact that it serves as a bulwark against prostitution and the largely beneficial effect it has on women's health and family planning, and instead it stresses the importance of the couple and the nuclear family. Whatever the other merits of such opposition, the Church's championing of the rights of women has become an important factor in Kenyan life. In a commissioned report to OXFAM on the family-planning needs of people in rural Kenya, Gill Shepherd has drawn attention to an unexpected spin-off effect of the Church's emphasis on male-female equality. With the drift of men to the cities breaking traditional male tribal arrangements, rural women are learning to co-operate more and more effectively.

> The message is put over, not only through the extensive support given to women's groups, but also in Church teaching. Priests teach that men and women are equal in the sight of God and certain Church rituals have incorporated this equality. For instance, at Church weddings, there are not only speeches by the husband's father and the wife's father (as in the pre-Christian ceremony) but also nowadays from the husband's mother and the wife's mother as well. Since the authority of the Church has in various ways taken over the religious authority that the tribal elders had in pre-colonial times, such details are not seen as trivial.[4]

George's fourth wife, Monica, is a member of one of the local women's self-help groups that are becoming a feature of rural Kenya. The group members, made up almost entirely of women from polygamous marriages whose husbands work at a distant town, run a fishing business and own their own boat. It is not the most propitious time to be trying to establish one's financial independence, given the economic recession and the faltering Kenyan economy. Yet it is difficult to dispute the view, powerfully argued at the 1985 UN Decade for Women Conference in Nairobi by many Third World delegates, that only through acquiring economic power can women hope to achieve sexual equality and a balanced relationship with men. The polygamous structure of traditional Kenyan society and the fragmented, casual and unstructured sexual contacts of urban Nairobi both militate against women; both seem to meet needs of Kenyan males. Not surprisingly, women in both situations seek change.

Given female dependence on men, particularly in traditional societies such as Kenya, Egypt and parts of Japan, it is tempting to explain women's preoccupation with fidelity in terms of a lack of security, of self-esteem, of self-confidence. In this respect it is interesting to note that there is a literature which supports the view that there are important sex differences both in the source of sexual jealousy and in the subjective experience of jealousy. Psychoanalyst Theodore Reik has claimed that men concentrate more on sexual aspects of infidelity whereas women are more concerned with the loss of relationship and of security. Men, according to Theodore Reik, not infrequently torture themselves with vivid images of their partners engaged in sexual activity with a rival. Women, conversely, express more concern about the possibility of losing their partner and the resultant insecurity, combined with the fear of the alienation of the partner's affections. Two British psychiatrists, Paul Mullen and Lara Maack, in a recent thorough review of jealousy and aggression,[5] concluded that from the little evidence available sexual jealousy does indeed appear to be less common in women than in men and, in general, jealousy does correlate positively with low self-esteem. Male self-esteem being bound up with public status and sexual prowess, and female self-esteem, in traditional societies at least, being tied to the approval and support of men, it would seem reasonable to expect that fidelity for women is bound up less with sexual than with social and personal considerations than it is for men.

A more socio-biological explanation of the importance of fidelity, particularly for men, relates to the assumption that without sexual constancy on the part of their womenfolk men could never be certain of the paternity of their partner's children. Jealousy is in the genes because it is evolutionarily adaptive. The male who chases away a rival ensures that his own genes will survive into the next generation. Such an explanation, however, does depend on a recognition of the link between sexual intercourse and pregnancy, a link which is now of course common knowledge but was not always known. A celebrated anthropological study of the inhabitants of the Trobriand Islands in the Pacific by Bronislaw Malinowski in the 1920s suggests that such an explanation may be too simple. The Trobrianders, Malinowski noted, have a permissive attitude towards premarital sex but after marriage such an attitude dramatically changes. Then the male can kill his wife if he discovers that she has been unfaithful whereas the wife is helpless in the face of her husband's adulterous behaviour. But the Trobrianders do not know that sexual intercourse leads to pregnancy, or at least they did not know when Malinowski studied them. They believed that pregnancy occurred when a spirit entered an opening in the woman's body and that this most commonly occurred when she was swimming. Males who had been away for a year or more on fishing expeditions would not react adversely to the pregnancies of their wives. The fact that very young children in this society engaged in copulation yet did not become pregnant only reduced still further the chance that the Trobrianders would make the association between sex and pregnancy.

So why did the double standard about infidelity operate here, too? And why to this day is it acceptable for a Japanese male to frequent hostess-bars and the brothels of Bangkok and Seoul whereas his wife must maintain an aura of maidenly submissiveness and public virtue? And why is adultery a punishable offence for Egyptian women wherever they commit it, whereas only if they besmirch the family hearth are Egyptian men treated similarly? And why is it that Kenyan males who boast of their sexual athleticism and collect their wives like trophies regard female extramarital activity with loathing and brand such women whores?

American sociologist Ira Reiss suggests that the explanation must be sought in the relationship between the female and the child-bearing role rather than between the male and the issue of paternity. Virtually every culture defines child-bearing and rearing as activities which require close attention and supervision. Extramarital relationships, particularly undertaken by married women, can be seriously disruptive. But does not male infidelity pose a potential threat to the effective carrying out of important and valued male duties and activities? Reiss answers that since men are in power they make the rules and the rules restrict others. In fact, to an extent, particularly in Japanese society, male sexual activity is seen as potentially disruptive to the more serious requirements of Japanese industrial expansion and is tolerated only by being rendered peripheral and recreational, becoming truly 'a bit on the side'.

Fidelity within marital relationships is still highly valued in Britain. In 1981, in a survey undertaken by the multinational European Value Systems Group and described as one of the largest surveys on values ever undertaken on a worldwide basis, 78 per cent of the British sample agreed with the seventh commandment – 'Thou shalt not commit adultery' – a far higher proportion than in any other European country. However, respondents believed that only 25 per cent of other people abided by the commandment and it was clear that infidelity within marriage is an important source of problems.

On the basis of two surveys of British values and beliefs in 1950 and 1969, British social anthropologist Geoffrey Gorer suggested that infidelity appeared to be more important in the late 1960s as a cause of unhappiness within marriage than it had been some twenty years previously – but so too was jealousy. Only 5 per cent of the 1969 sample, evenly distributed by age, sex and social class, actually felt that faithfulness was not now so important and men appeared more concerned with sexual fidelity than women. In a *Sunday Times*/MORI poll conducted in 1982, over 70 per cent of eighteen- to twenty-four-year-olds, over 80 per cent of sixty-five-year-olds and over two-thirds of the entire sample felt that adultery was morally wrong. Fidelity, closely followed by mutual respect, understanding, tolerance and happy sexual relations, were the attributes most frequently considered necessary for a successful marriage, according to the European Values study. At the top of the list of items constituting sufficient grounds for divorce were the persistent infidelity of either partner, violence, falling out of love and excessive drinking.

This emphasis on the importance of fidelity persists despite the increase in life expectation following improvements in public health which now means that many couples face an undissolved marital relationship spanning forty or fifty years, compared with the fifteen or twenty years experienced by their not so remote ancestors. Despite this increase in the expected duration of marriage, there is still a persistent tendency to view the marriage that ends in divorce as a failure.

So is fidelity a realistic ambition of twentieth-century marriage? Yes, say the Islamic fundamentalists of Egypt, religious idealists for whom marital constancy and sexual faithfulness remain the driving aspirations of the marital relationship and the foundation stones of trust and stability within society. Yes, say traditional Kenyans, but it is a qualified yes; you must circumscribe the natural male need for sexual relations within the disciplined, structured, socially responsible institution of polygamy. Yes, say the permissive Californians, but for them sexual fidelity and feelings of jealousy are psychological hang-ups reflecting male potency fears and female dependence; true fidelity involves a degree of intimacy so total that it involves sharing one's sexual needs with others outside the marital relationship while working through the residual feelings of guilt and insecurity within it. The resultant tolerance is achieved, if indeed it is achieved in more than just a handful of unusual marriages, by dethroning sexual intimacy from its high position as the marker of marital and personal commitment and making it just another recreational pursuit like surfing, golfing or eating. But as leisure is so important in California, sexual activity retains its standing as a serious endeavour, to be worked on, improved and made the subject of manuals, guides and workshops. The biggest single threat to the sex-as-leisure stance is when it becomes part of a loving, absorbing, intimate relationship.

What does appear unarguable is that over the last twenty years there has been a detectable move away from the double standards of male and female behaviour. The advent of wide-spread birth control has split procreation from intercourse. Extramarital sex has been proclaimed as an aid to marriage and attacked as a betrayal of it. The battle is joined between those who insist that the liberation of sex from negative and inhibit-ing attitudes is a mark of progress and those who see in the elevation of sex as recreation no more than a return to licen-tiousness and lust. Are these changes in sexual behaviour, asks psychiatrist Jack Dominian,

> . . . a mere swing of the pendulum familiar in history or are we witnessing one of those key periods of humanity where a real advance in human understanding is being made about sexual activity?

Meanwhile, the goals of fidelity and indissolubility continue to exercise their appeal to the great majority of those who enter the matrimonial state. Expectations of marriage have rarely been so great. The institution groans under the weight of the emotional, social and physical satisfactions demanded of it. It is hardly surprising that fidelity gives under the strain, hardly surprising either that the indissolubility of marriage is looking distinctly shaky as the winds of divorce gather force.

6   GROUNDS FOR DIVORCE

In Egypt, the former cultural attaché at the Egyptian Embassy in Washington arrived home to discover that her husband had divorced her in her absence and without her knowledge after a marriage lasting eighteen years. All he had had to do was present himself before a *mazun*, or marriage registrar, in the presence of two supporting witnesses and declare that the marriage was over. That is the law. In Sweden, divorce petitioners of either sex do not have to state a reason. As long as there are no children involved, the divorce is instant. If there are children, there is merely a six-month cooling-off period. That is the law. In Hungary, too, there are few legal barriers to divorce and the country boasts one of the highest rates in the world. Financial support to ex-wives is guaranteed by the simple expedient of deducting from the ex-husband's wages the amount of alimony and giving it to the ex-wife. In Japan, divorce legislation is likewise liberal but the rate, by international standards, is modest. There, divorce is still a somewhat shameful business and erring spouses are persuaded by a mixture of emotional blackmail and peer pressure to return to the marital fold. Italy, likewise, has a very low divorce rate although divorce in that predominantly Catholic country has been legally available since 1974. One deterrent may well be the mandatory period of separation before a divorce can be granted: five years in the case of an uncontested divorce, seven years if one of the parties objects.

And what of divorce in Britain? The ideal of lifelong monogamy, at the root of the Christian tradition of marriage, has underpinned English legislation on marriage and divorce. Sexual fidelity, for centuries, had been at the core of divorce legislation but it was only in 1857 that the need for a divorcing couple to obtain a specific Act of Parliament was abolished. As recently as 1922, a dual standard applied whereby a wife's adultery was considered sufficient grounds for divorce whereas a husband's adultery had to be aggravated by some further offence, such as cruelty. Divorce changes in 1938 extended the accepted grounds for divorce to include desertion, cruelty or insanity while the Divorce Reform Act (1969) changed the grounds for divorce to 'irretrievable breakdown of marriage' as indicated by desertion, separation, unreasonable behaviour or intolerable adultery.

Prior to the First World War, the annual number of divorces never exceeded 10,000 in England and Wales. A substantial increase in the wake of the Second World War did occur but the numbers fell back during the 1960s. Such was the stability of the rates in the 1950s that two analysts of divorce trends, G. Rowntree and N. H. Carrier, concluded in 1958 that divorces would be most likely to continue to run at a rate of around 30,000 a year for the foreseeable future. Within a decade of that prediction, divorce rates were beginning an inexorable rise which was to see them top 100,000 by the early 1970s and reach over 150,000 by the 1980s.

'If you don't succeed at first, remarry,' might appear to sum up contemporary attitudes towards the institution. Of the 158,000 divorce decrees made absolute in 1984, one in five involved couples in which at least one partner had been divorced before, compared with one in eleven in 1971. The number of divorce petitions filed in England and Wales increased sharply after October 1984 because of a change in the law which allowed people to petition for divorce after only one year of marriage whereas under former legislation only in exceptional circumstances could a petition be presented before the third wedding anniversary.

In 1984, about three in every four decrees awarded went to petitioning wives. Their most frequent justification was unreasonable behaviour on the part of their husbands (this was the cause cited by 46 per cent of wives granted decrees). The reason most cited by petitioning husbands was their wives' adultery (43 per cent of husbands granted decrees gave this as the reason). The older a couple are when they marry, the less likely they are to divorce. Spouses who marry in their teens are twice as likely to divorce as those who marry between twenty and twenty-four. Thirty-five per cent of British divorces in 1984 involved wives who had married in their teens. Relatively few men marry aged twenty or less but about half the divorces in 1984 were to men who were aged between twenty and twenty-four at the time of their marriage.

Patterns of divorce in the United States closely resemble trends in Britain. Divorce hardly increased at all during the period 1920–65. Many marriages were made in haste during the war while others were exposed to immense strain through enforced separation. Also, couples who stayed together during the economic crises of the 1930s broke up a decade later – there is persuasive evidence that divorce goes up with an improvement in economic conditions. (In part, this may be due to the fact that more people can afford to go through the legal processes involved.) The divorce rate in America then began to rise during the late 1960s and by 1978 the rate was running at twenty-two per 1000 marriages per year, almost double the British rate.

There is nothing particularly British, therefore, about rising divorce rates. Indeed because the phenomenon is apparently a very general one, it is unlikely that the simple explanation that legislative 'easing' of divorce is the culprit can be sustained. Changes in the law do not follow a common pattern in the countries concerned. Nor can the rise in divorce rates be seen as a movement away from marriage as an institution. The proportion of the eligible population that marries is, as we have seen (Chapter 2), as high as it has ever been while the number of remarriages has paralleled that of divorce.

What appears to be happening is that we are moving towards a pattern of two or more marriages in a lifetime. But remarriages are no more likely to be enduring. Marriages involving spouses who have been married before are about twice as likely to end in divorce as those that involve partners who have had no previous marital partners. Indeed, current remarriage rates in Britain are such that about one in three of all marriages are a second or subsequent one for at least one of the spouses.

Wherever we look marriage appears vulnerable. Yet the expectation that marriage will prove indissoluble remains an entrenched one in the minds of most people embarking on married life. As we have seen, changes in life expectancy mean that a couple embarking on marriage today can expect an undissolved relationship to span forty or even fifty years. Yet, despite this change in the potential length of marriage and the wide-spread incidence of divorce, there is still a deeply engrained view of marriage ending in divorce as a 'failed' marriage.

Lovelaw was interested in the way other societies, which do not necessarily share the Judaeo-Christian vision of marriage, cope with the question of marital breakdown. What is the breaking-point for married couples in, for example, Islamic Egypt, communist Hungary, capitalist Japan? What systems do these societies provide for divorce? Do stricter divorce laws maintain marriages or are economic conditions and social attitudes more potent predictors of marital durability?

In Egypt, *Lovelaw* interviewed Dr Afaz Mahfouz, an Egyptian lawyer who married her husband when she was nineteen and he was six years older, and whose instant divorce was referred to at the beginning of this chapter. They had been childhood friends, studied together in Paris and shared eighteen years of marriage. While she was in America, as a cultural attaché at the Egyptian Embassy in Washington, she learned from her husband that he had become involved with another woman. He insisted that he did not want to divorce his wife given the length and satisfactions of their marriage but he did want her to accept the other woman. When Dr Mahfouz made it plain that she could not tolerate this twentieth-century equivalent of polygamy, her husband promised to end the liaison and returned to Cairo. Dr Mahfouz followed a few weeks later, to be told by mutual friends that her husband had divorced her.

Dr Mahfouz explains that there are three ways to obtain a divorce in Egypt. The first involves going to court. In most instances, it is the wife who chooses this option for reasons that will become obvious. Before the court, she argues her petition on the basis of a specified breach of the marital contract. In practice, few women seek a divorce in Egypt, even if unhappily married, for the simple reason that the low economic status of most Egyptian women makes it difficult for a divorcee to survive. The judges are always men and they are known to be prejudiced against women who petition for divorce. The second way to obtain a divorce is for the husband to exercise his right under Egyptian and Islamic law and divorce her without her consent. The husband goes before a divorce registrar (*mazun*) and simply registers his divorce before two witnesses while promising the *mazun* that he, and the registrar, will notify the wife. No reasons have to be provided although the *mazun* is supposed to try to persuade the husband to consider possible attempts at reconciliation. But if the husband insists, as happened in Dr Mahfouz's case, the divorce is granted. The third process of divorce involves the mutual consent of both parties. Husband and wife go before the *mazun* to express their desire to separate and register their divorce.

The second option is the commonest but despite its relative simplicity it has not led to a flood of divorces. The main reason for this appears to be economic. Under Islamic law, marriage is first and foremost a contract. Like any contract, there are conditions. In theory, an Egyptian woman can protect her circumstances by drawing up a marriage contract which would give her the right to travel without her husband's permission, to work outside the home and to obtain a divorce if she felt the marriage had broken down irretrievably. In practice, it is a rare woman who does so. Insisting on such contracts would cause opposition not merely from the husband-to-be and his family but from the men within the family of the prospective bride. What restricts the husband to some extent in his search for divorce is not the law but the fact that on divorce he would have to pay back his marriage dowry or *mahr*. This is money or property which the wife brings to the marriage but which must be returned to the wife if her husband dies or divorces her. The dowry is related to the wealth of both parties and could be the equivalent of several years' salary. But it is not much of a restraint in practice. For one thing, the whole notion of the dowry is weak and weakening. For another, the sums may be calculated on the basis of amounts agreed at the time of the wedding, ten, fifteen or, as in Dr Mahfouz's case, eighteen years previously. Inflation will have reduced them to nominal amounts.

It is true that under Islamic law, women, including married women, exercise independent powers of ownership. Dr Mahfouz owned property in her own name. It is very common for even poor women to have a little land of their own. This right is recognised by Islam. But for the Egyptian woman without anything divorce can be ruinous. *Lovelaw* filmed a scene from a famous, Muslim fundamentalists would say infamous, Egyp-

> *If we show men the truth [about marriage and divorce] it will get through to them. I remember when I made that film [I Want a Solution] I asked the director to do it. Then he read the script, the story, and he laughed. He had a certain smile on his face, a sarcastic one. Then I asked him to go to the divorce court and see for himself. Believe me, he went twice and he became very convinced of the need for this film. Then I told him, 'Please, just make it, tell the truth.'*
>
> *Faten Hamama*

tian film, *I Want a Solution*. In it, a middle-aged woman from one of the provinces, after twenty years of unhappy marriage, seeks a divorce. The part is played by Egyptian film star Faten Hamama, ex-wife of Omar Sharif, for whom the film is a personal statement concerning the plight of Egyptian women. The woman she plays in the film explains that at the time she was married she could not choose her husband. It was her father who did the choosing. After the first year of marriage, she went to her father to say she could not go on. Her husband was an alcoholic, was persistently unfaithful and physically abused her. The suggestion of a separation provoked shock and scandal in her own family. The marriage had to go on. A child was born and reared with much effort. After twenty years the wife could take it no longer and went to court. In humiliating detail, she was forced to go through the intimate details of her marriage, one by one. In the end, the judge ruled against her. Her husband had done all that was asked of him in the marital contract – he had provided his wife with all her material needs including food, clothing, a roof over her head, a child. So divorce was refused. She appealed and after a legal process lasting over four years her appeal was turned own.

In another story in the same film, the divorce double standard is neatly illustrated. It concerns an elderly lady who had lived with her husband for thirty years and had been a good wife. She could not, however, bear him any children. Then her husband decided that he would take to himself a new wife and promptly divorced her. He gave her what Egyptian law insists is given to childless wives on divorce – one year's alimony. On the completion of that year, the divorced wife was penniless. She had no money, no property, no home. In late middle age, she had to take up the job of a maid in a great house. Attempts to obtain legal redress failed utterly.

In 1979, minor reforms to marital law were introduced by the late President Anwar Sadat. These were popularly named after his wife, Jihan Sadat, who had personally championed them. The Jihan's law, which, the Sadat government reassured suspicious fundamentalist religious leaders, was compatible with the teachings of the Koran and Islamic Shari'ah law, included a requirement for a husband to inform a wife that she had been divorced and for her to be able to petition for divorce if her husband took another wife or if she found out that he was already married. But the most radical change was the reform which allowed the divorced woman to stay in the family home while the children were still legally in the care of their mother. This legal age was also raised from nine to eleven for boys and from eleven to fifteen, or even until marriage in some cases, for girls.

For a few months before Egypt's constitutional court considered it, the law was the target of fundamentalists who attacked it regularly in the mosques as heretical. The aim of the law had been to cut down on divorces, limit polygamy and provide divorced women with a minimum of resources. Some magistrates refused to apply it on grounds of conscience and the constitutional court annulled it. On 18 May 1985 the six-year-old reform was finally buried with an official judgement restoring husbands' full Islamic legal rights over their wives. This decision meant that Egyptian men can once more take up to four wives without having to tell any of them of the existence of the others and can divorce them again at will. And divorced wives lost their rights to the family home.

Conservative judges insisted that the Jihan's law created more problems than it had solved. Many women were alleged to have taken advantage of it to swindle their husbands out of their homes and substantial amounts of alimony. A judge in the civil court of the Cairo working-class district of Shubra-El-Kheima was quoted as saying that the number of matrimonial disputes had almost doubled since the Jihan's law was enacted.

Lovelaw filmed a divorce application in a Cairo court. It concerned an old lady who was seeking the court's assistance in her efforts to persude her ex-husband to pay her alimony. After forty-five years of marriage he had left her for another woman

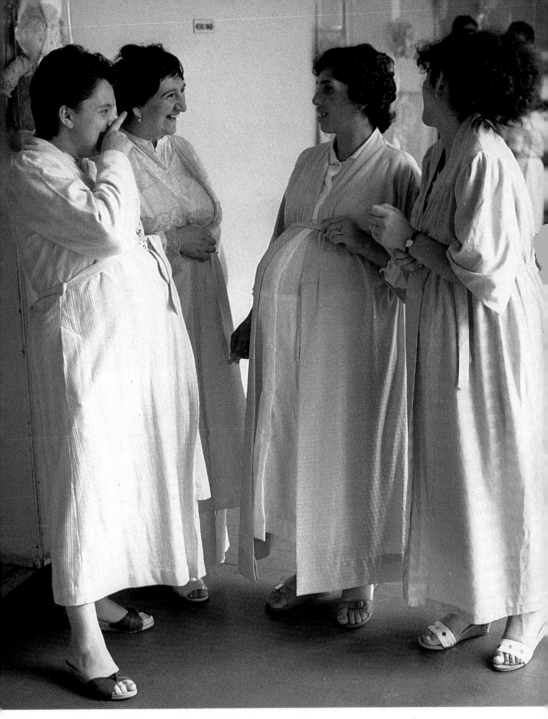

Pregnant Italian women share a joke. The birth rate in Italy is one of the lowest in the world, but so is contraceptive use. This is due to the influence of the Roman Catholic Church

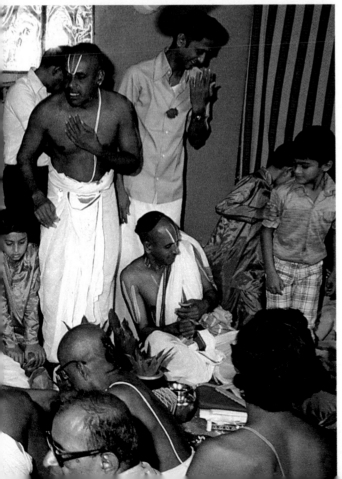

Far left A divorce court in Cairo. Women judges are not permitted in Egypt

Left If an Egyptian husband and wife agree that they want a divorce they go to the local registrar's office and simply sign a divorce document

Below A Brahmin couple celebrate the husband's sixtieth birthday by repeating their wedding ceremony – this time for the benefit of the grown-up children

Above A Chinese
woman working in a
factory in Peking.
Throughout the world
women are
increasingly entering
the workplaces
traditionally
associated with men

Below Top Egyptian actress Faten Hamama (former wife of Omar Sharif) describes her starring role in a famous film about the plight of an Egyptian woman seeking divorce. The film I Want a Solution is said to have been a major influence in an attempt to reform the divorce laws

小美山とも子さん(15)

03-264-4000まで

田中ナツ子(42)

03-264-4000まで

公開捜

公開捜

03-264-4000

Above Amending
family photographs
after a divorce by
airbrushing out the
absent partner is big
business in California

Left A popular
phone-in television
show which attempts
to trace runaway
children and husbands
through inducing guilt

English children
learning about the
physical aspects of
love. In Britain
teachers still feel
ambivalent about sex
education

and was now paying her nothing. The old lady revealed that she was fifteen years old when she married and that she had known no other men,

> I stayed married for twenty years and gave birth to four children. His family hated him and boycotted him. I mean they isolated us. I, therefore, sold my jewellery and fixed him a job in a factory. The marriage lasted forty-five years . . . I sold my property and supported him and he climbed over my head. Later when he got a pay rise from the factory, he went and got married to another woman and she gave birth to a child. Then he sent me the divorce paper. I never saw the person who ratified the divorce. I never attended anything. I looked and there was the postman telling me, 'Take this, it's a letter.' I open the letter. I find it is a divorce.

The old woman's lawyer explained that in Egypt the wife can claim alimony but the precise amount is based on the circumstances of the case. She had already obtained a judgement whereby her former husband had to pay her a sum of five hundred Egyptian pounds in a lump sum but he promptly appealed on the basis that he was a poor man and owned nothing. The lawyer insisted that he was a rich man who owned two properties but had arranged to have the properties registered in his second wife's name so that he could appear in court as impoverished. The case had already lasted a year and seemed certain to last at least a further six months. Meanwhile the old woman remained penniless and was losing hope.

Dr Mahfouz points out that suing for divorce and alimony can be a profoundly humiliating experience for a woman. Muslim law demands that the husband be the provider in the marriage and even when the wife has wealth of her own the husband takes full financial responsibility. If he fails to fulfil his contractual financial duties then he can be sued for divorce. Likewise, if he fails to fulfil his sexual duties he can also be divorced. But these remain the only grounds. The wife who is materially provided for but whose husband is physically abusing her or is promiscuous can only argue sexual failure as grounds for divorce. She has to show that they did not make love for a certain period of time and there are different interpretations of what constitutes an appropriately frustrating period of abstinence. Seeking a divorce on such grounds is shameful for most Egyptian women who have to provide evidence of a highly intimate kind for a judiciary which is entirely male.

By contrast, Japanese divorce law seems extremely tolerant. About 90 per cent of all divorces there are enacted by mutual consent, 9 per cent are settled by arbitration and only 1 per cent are taken through a court of law. Divorce by mutual consent involves no more than the completion by husband and wife of a form bearing their names, dates of birth, addresses and suchlike which is then forwarded to a particular public office. On acceptance by the divorce office of the form, the marriage is dissolved. An arbitrated divorce is one in which the couple cannot agree and a member of an arbitration committee tries to find points of agreement or of compromise to achieve a divorce settlement. In the event that no agreement can be reached by arbitration, the case goes to court for a legal ruling.

Japan has always had a somewhat liberal attitude towards divorce. In pre-war Japan, there was what was known as 'dismissal divorce' whereby a husband could divorce his wife if she could not give birth to a son and heir or because she could not get on with his mother. Such divorces were common. Japanese divorce expert, Madoka Yoriko, told *Lovelaw* that the feeling still remains in Japanese women's minds that they are the vulnerable ones when it comes to divorce. Japanese women find going to court shameful. In addition, when faced with divorce they are so distressed that they cannot begin to take steps to protect themselves. As a result and despite the high proportion of mutually agreed divorces, Japanese women often end up disadvantaged as a consequence of divorce. In 1979, a survey carried out by the Japanese Ministry of Health and Welfare, which examined the distribution of assets and compensation payments in agreed divorces, found that half of the husbands obtained divorces without paying a penny to their wives. Of those who actually paid, most parted with a sum of money which would have been just enough to permit the wife to live on for two or three months, long enough to leave the marital home and find a flat. The great majority of divorced mothers, Madoka Yoriko reminded us, look after the children,

At present 70 per cent of divorcing couples have children under twenty years old and 70 per cent of them are looked after by their mothers. Amongst these mothers, half have not received any money in compensation or their share of assets from their ex-husbands. You may wonder about the costs of bringing up children but, sad to say, while 30 per cent of divorced husbands pay them for about six months or a year, that is it. At present, there are 460,000 divorced mothers with children in Japan and only 10 per cent of them are receiving the costs of bringing up the children from their ex-husbands.

Prior to the Second World War, Japanese wives did not have the right to the custody of the children. It was only after the war that the situation was changed. On divorce, both parents have to decide which of them takes custody. Up to about 1969 it was overwhelmingly the fathers who looked after the children. Even though the law had changed with the ending of the war, people's minds had not. Many believed that women were inferior to men and therefore would not be able to look after children on their own, or educate them. In addition, women had even less economic power than they have now.

At the present time there are very few fathers who insist on looking after the children following divorce. A survey conducted by Madoka Yoriko revealed that only 30 per cent of Japanese fathers had maintained any contact with their children after divorce, and if they had it was almost entirely due to the fact that the mothers had encouraged the fathers to share the task of bringing up the children. In Japan, the divorce expert explained, once people are divorced and separated, most believe that it is best for the children's sake to leave them alone and not to disturb them. Mothers and children are now seen as the natural unit. Earlier, when the children had been seen largely as heirs to the house and inheritors of the family property, custody devolved to fathers. With the weakening of property ties and the slow growth of emphasis on emotional issues, the mother has taken over from the father as the natural custodian of the children. In addition, many fathers feel that if they were to keep in touch with their offspring they would be expected to pay the costs of bringing them up which many of them do not want to do. Madoka Yoriko's survey found more cases of fathers not wishing to see their children than of mothers who did not want their children to see their fathers.

The major motive for Japanese divorce is economic. Gradually, other reasons are coming to the fore, for example, wives feel their aims in life have become different from their husbands', or that husbands have taken other lovers. But while such causes are increasing, economic factors remain the biggest single cause of Japanese divorce. This means, declares Madoka Yoriko, that people still believe that women's happiness depends on men and the main condition for making women happy is men's financial strength. There are many Japanese women who eventually tire of husbands who do not possess the requisite earning power and they divorce them. However, the problem of alimony and family support still remains.

For the moment, the Japanese divorce rate, at four per 1000 marriages per year, is one-third of the British rate and about one-sixth of the American rate. Yasuhiko Yuzawa, a Japanese professor of the sociology of law, in an analysis in 1981 of divorce trends, sees little evidence of a significant rise yet. The actual number of divorces did rise sharply from 77,000 in 1965 to 132,000 in 1978 but these figures are crude and are not adjusted for the changing structure of post-war Japanese society. When such an adjustment is undertaken, the rate of four divorces per 1000 marriages is higher than the 1960s rate but is lower than for any year between 1945 and 1955. The current Japanese rates are by no means the highest since the war. In fact, increases in the number of divorces have been surpassed by increases in the overall number of married couples. Of particular importance is the fact that vast numbers of people from the so-called 'baby boom' generation married about eight to ten years ago and are now within the period of greatest risk (divorced couples in Japan average about seven years of marriage). Thus there are good statistical grounds for expecting an upsurge in Japanese divorce. In the area of divorce, concludes Yasuhiko Yuzawa, 'the changes in Japan are extremely minor compared with those in Western countries'.

Another explanation of Japan's low divorce rate in the presence of 'liberal' divorce laws relates to the role of shame in Japanese society. Up to the Second World War, the family system was based on the ie or ancestral family unit. The household was continued by the eldest son and, indeed, it was the general rule for him to remain at home with his parents even after marriage. The family, which included grandparents, was the vital element in the socialisation of children. The majority of pre-war Japanese grew up in ie based on a direct line of ancestral descent and were exposed to what Professor Tadashi Fukutake, head of the Social Development Research Institute in

> There are many women who say that because their husbands provide them with the money to live on they don't want to divorce even if their husbands have for many years been having affairs, or have often been sleeping out, or have come home only once a week or once a month, or if they sleep apart and never have sexual intercourse, or they don't have dinner together at all, or there is no conversation between them because their husbands only speak when absolutely necessary. And it is not only because of money but maybe, for example, because she is the wife of a senior manager . . . or because they have a detached house in Tokyo, because of all these reasons, they cannot throw their present life away. When, for example, they have lived solely as so-and-so's wife, or little such-and-such's mother, they wouldn't have any identity of their own after divorce. Therefore, for these people, their anxiety about losing all these things is extremely high, and not only for financial reasons, but also because of the worry of losing status in society, they insist they can't get divorced. True, some people who come here to ask for advice have been in distress for a long time. Their cheeks look sunken because of worry but even so they say they can't get divorced. Also some husbands do not want to get divorced because it might damage their promotion chances or because people may consider them peculiar if they get divorced.
>
> Madoka Yoriko
> Japanese divorce counsellor

Tokyo, calls the 'culture of shame'. This culture was fostered by mothers and grandmothers who were constantly concerned with the praise or censure of those around them. Emphasis was not placed on right or wrong, 'but on behaving in such a way as to avoid shame and ridicule from others'. Disciplined by this type of upbringing, many Japanese developed the view that the safest path to take was to respect the authority of the head of the household and other authority figures in their immediate environment and to conform with the behaviour of their peers.

Post-war changes in Japanese society have altered much of this. There is, in the opinion of Japanese observers, a weakening of family discipline and there is confusion over how best to make the transition to a method of character formation in which strict imposed discipline in the early stages of a child's life is replaced by an increasing amount of individual self-discipline as the child grows older. The result, according to Professor Fukutake, is that Japanese children

. . . either rebel or become self-scorning and self-centred. Alternatively, they may succumb to apathy and conform meekly to their parents' wishes. Apart from apathetic conformity, however, the result is likely to be a widening gulf between the generations.

Yet the 'culture of shame' still exercises a powerful influence over Japanese behaviour. Divorce, for example, is still seen as a stigmatising and shameful disgrace, as is desertion of families by husbands or wives. This sense of shame can be utilised to force wives and husbands who have simply had too much of a marriage and who have just walked out to come back and accept their lot. A particularly popular show on Japanese television exploits this sense of shame in a most potent fashion. *Lovelaw* filmed the live transmission of one such programme in a Nippon Television studio. Spouses stand in front of large, blown-up pictures of their runaway partners and appeal to viewers for help to track them down. Viewers phone the studio with information. Errant husbands and frustrated wives are dragged to telephones. Tearful reunions are arranged. Children weep. The show's host wraps it up for the evening and Japanese viewers go back to their task of getting through the day.

On Nippon Television's *Public Search*, the hunt is on for Mr Takao Uchiyama, a twenty-nine-year-old farmer who left his home on 5 April 1985 and never returned. The reason for his disappearance was an affair with a twenty-one-year-old woman. Mr Uchiyama's wife is in her last month of pregnancy, the television show's host tells viewers, and the missing man's father is particularly concerned about his son's behaviour and his daughter-in-law's predicament. As for Mr Uchiyama's whereabouts, he is thought to be in the vicinity of Okayama, working in a sports shop.

The two other subjects of the programme are a fifteen-year-old girl who has been missing for a year, having eloped with a forty-six-year-old man who has a record of 'staying in motels with other junior high school students', and a forty-three-year-old woman who left her husband after arguing with him about the affairs they both appear to have been having.

The television network's telephone numbers are broadcast and the host then whiles away the time by discussing the details of the separations and desertions with key relatives of the missing trio. Mr Uchiyama's career as a farmer is analysed, and we learn that five days after he disappeared, his daughter, Hitomi, entered nursery school. The host expresses the view that, 'It is beyond belief that, despite knowing what was coming and also that his wife was due to have a baby soon, anybody would run off with another woman.' A film clip of the area in which the Uchiyamas live and work is then shown, as are clothes similar to the ones he was wearing on the last day he was seen. The screw of shame is tightened with the revelation that five-year-old Hitomi has stopped going to nursery school as she is anxious that her mother will disappear next and a further film clip of the Uchiyama family 'coping' is then shown.

Then little Hitomi herself is interviewed and great emphasis is laid on the fact that the poor child cries for her Daddy every night and asks for him every morning. The pregnant wife expresses the doleful view that it would be better if the expected baby were never to be born and by the time the whole presentation has been completed Mr Uchiyama, if he has been watching, should be a mass of quivering shame and embarrassment. Then the telephones start to ring. Mr Uchiyama has been seen in a local sports shop in Fukuoka. A local man who knows him telephones. Then Mr Uchiyama telephones in a pitiful and repentant state. Reconciliations are arranged in time for the credits to roll and the host waves viewers goodbye with the promise that next week at the same time *Public Search* will be there to help all good Japanese to maintain their sense of duty and honour their responsibilities.

Throughout the programme, the emphasis has been on the shame attached to Mr Uchiyama's desertion as a father rather than as a husband, reflecting the relative values placed on these two aspects of the role of a man in Japanese marriage. Shame also attaches to Japanese wives who cannot cope with their role in Japanese marriage and leave. One such was Mieko Tanaka, an artist living on the beautiful Izu peninsula. She married at twenty-five, a typical Japanese-style arranged marriage. For two and a half years, she struggled to make it work but family tensions and marked incompatibilities led her to seek a divorce. Now she finds herself socially ostracised. Her family blame her, believing that her divorce has brought shame upon the family name. The villagers refuse to talk to both her and her family and treat her like a criminal. Shortly after her divorce, she had a mental breakdown and was in hospital for three months. Seven years after the divorce, Mieko is still not reabsorbed into normal Japanese society. Divorce may be legal and, by the standards of other cultures, easy to obtain, but social disapproval and pressures on couples to remain together for public appearances are immense. Separation, revealing private difficulties to the public gaze, is no more acceptable.

In Italy, divorce has only been legally available since 1970 and still carries a social stigma. Its introduction was fiercely opposed by the Roman Catholic Church and certain checks and balances were built into the legislation to meet the constant accusation that the legislation undermined family life and was a Casanova's charter. The most celebrated check of all is that there is a mandatory minimum period of five years' separation if both partners agree before a divorce is finalised and this period becomes seven years if one of the couple is contesting the application and/or there are children. Critics of British divorce often argue for a separation period in order to exhaust every attempt to save and restore a marriage before accepting dissolution; so how does this proviso work in Italy?

Not very well, it would appear. The period of separation was a concession to the Christian Democrats but there is now an all-party move to reduce the period to one year in cases where there are no children and both parties agree to divorce and three years if there are children. Five years during which both partners work hard at reconciliation sounds fine in theory. In practice it can be a recipe for a bloody war!

An additional problem concerns the precise social standing of the separated person waiting for a divorce. For Leila Cafasi the period of separation was extremely traumatic. When she was twenty-one she had married Emmanuel, the son of an aristocrat from Calabria. In 1979, Emmanuel made an application for a 'judicial separation'. What began as a mutual decision to separate escalated badly and five years of legal argument, court appearances and unpleasant wrangling passed before Leila obtained custody of their four children.

But worse than the bureaucratic delay was what appeared to Leila Cafasi to be the discriminatory way the procedures regarding separation and divorce are undertaken in contemporary Italy,

For instance, my first meeting with one of the Presidents of the Court was utterly traumatic. He was a man who, although calm and unruffled, seemed absolutely to hate all women. His every expression was one of condemnation of women who were willing to agree to a separation instead of tolerating problems.

Divorce cases in Italy can and do drag on for years. Husbands and wives struggle to outdo each other in terms of the dishonourable things they are willing to contemplate. Wives are accused of living off alimony and of blackmailing reluctant husbands by threatening to reveal all they know (which in some cases may be a great deal) to the income tax office if alimony is not sufficient. Husbands cheat, evade and quibble over payments. The Italian solution of insisting on a mandatory period of 'cooling down' before divorce does not appear to be too successful.

In Hungary, divorce rates are high – 40 per cent of marriages end in the divorce courts. One in five Hungarian children grows up in a divorced family. The commonest time for divorce is about four to five years into the marriage, after the first child is born and about the time that the couple faces the full brunt of accommodation difficulties, lack of privacy and conflict about their respective roles. Divorce is frowned on and efforts are made by the courts to encourage conciliation. *Lovelaw* filmed one such conciliation hearing in one of the Budapest family law courts. The average tribunal is composed of three people and is presided over by a judge. All the judges in the family courts are women. In the case filmed, Bela Kovacs and his wife Szilvia were ostensibly discussing conciliation but in fact were vying for custody of their six-year-old son, Czaba.

The judge opened the proceedings by reminding the participants that the entire process was to be tape-recorded and that a record would be available from the court in two weeks. She then reviewed the salient features of the case, the fact that the petitioner, Szilvia, had asked for a dissolution of the marriage on the grounds of irretrievable breakdown due to the respondent, Bela, not having worked for a long time, having neglected his family and having involved his mother in an unhelpful way in the family's concerns. The respondent Bela had likewise asked for a dissolution but denied that he was to blame. Instead, he countered that it was his wife who had strayed from home, struck up intimate friendships with other men and neglected her child. Indeed, it was this neglect that had led him to involve his own mother in the upbringing of Czaba.

The court proceeded carefully to assess the evidence with a view to establishing the grounds for a conciliation attempt, the issue of divorce having been put aside. The issue of custody, however, inevitably arose for both Szilvia and Bela wished to know which of them would have Czaba should conciliation fail. Accordingly, social assessments of the marital home and of the home of Bela's mother were presented to the court and details of Czaba's nursery school attendance were made available. Further, the court listened to the expert opinions of a judicial psychologist in order to clarify the respective suitability of the parties and of the grandmother for educating the child.

The family home report reflected Hungary's infamous housing problems. The couple shared a one-roomed flat where they ate, slept, washed, cooked and attempted to conduct a life as married partners and parents. The psychological assessment of Szilvia's suitability as a mother revealed the fact that the girl herself was the child of divorced parents. She spent a considerable time as a child in the care of the State. Her husband

A Hungarian divorce tribunal. Unlike Egyptian courts where the judges are men, the judges in Hungary's family courts are always women

was the first man she ever really knew and she married him when he had a job (as a fireman) which he had since lost through unnamed difficulties. Her mother-in-law had been a constant problem and made plain her view of the unsuitability of Szilvia as a mother. Yes, Szilvia had had a boyfriend since the marriage began to break up but she denied that the relationship was serious and insisted that her child came first. The psychologist concluded that she had an unstable personality, the result of a psychosocial background of 'frequent adversity, emotional undermotivation and absence of stable attachments'. Her insecurity, emotional immaturity and impulsiveness and her lack of 'a suitable maternal image' suggested that she was, at the moment, unsuitable to bring up her child. Szilvia responded with spirit, and irrefutable logic, that if the fact that she was brought up in the care of the State disqualified her from parenthood then no one who was ever brought up in care would ever be legally qualified to rear a child! She countered too the suggestion that her mother-in-law would be a suitable alternative parent for her child by pointing out that the psychologist had actually drawn attention to the 'unusually strong mother-child relationship' between her husband and her mother-in-law. Would there not be a risk of an unusually strong grandmother-grandson relationship developing?

The court listened gravely to the arguments mounted by Bela and Szilvia and by their lawyers. Then Bela's lawyer revealed that his client was indeed anxious to try to solve the relationship with Szilvia and, in answer to the judge, Szilvia agreed to try again to bring up the little boy jointly and properly. The court decided to suspend the case for four months and the judge ended with a homily to the parents to give careful consideration to the needs and priorities of the child who had already suffered enough.

There was little evidence there of a flight to divorce. The reasons for divorce were predictable ones – disharmony, shortage of work, money and space, a hint or two of infidelity and more than a suggestion of insufficient awareness on the part of both husband and wife of the demands of child-rearing. And, of course, the traditional problem of the mother-in-law. Afterwards, Bela and Szilvia reflected on their eight years of marriage and the fact that for three years there had been troubles. Bela revealed that his mother was immensely jealous of her only son's marriage, having imagined that he would stay home with her forever. When his son was born, she tried to break the marriage up to regain her son together with her grandson. Outside the court and the inevitable adversarial atmosphere, Bela was able to reflect on these aspects of his predicament and admit to his own shortcomings. For her part, Szilvia realised that she did not handle the emotional strains and stresses of in-law trouble with much skill. And yes, they both said, such troubles are pretty common in Hungarian marriages.

The commonest reasons for divorce in Hungary include infidelity, alcohol abuse and a growing apart of the two parties. Two-thirds of all divorces occur within the first ten years of marriage. Accommodation difficulties and arguments related to them are a common and increasing cause of marital breakdown. The judge in the case filmed by *Lovelaw* provided her own perspective,

> I think the causes of divorce may be divided between the more deeply rooted social reasons that may be connected with the changing role of the family, the fact that most women now are wage-earners, the appearance of the two-job family . . . and what we here, at the court, perceive as tangible reasons – the parties speak of lack of mutual understanding, alienation – which may cover innumerable motives, from sexual problems to irresponsible, hasty marriages. A frequent reason for divorce suits is drinking, alcoholism which, in nearly every instance, results in offensive behaviour, even physical violence. Unfortunately, it has lately become more and more common that not the husband but the wife is guilty of frequent drunkenness. Common grounds for divorce are the housing problems or, at least, they give rise to the more immediate causes of the breakdown of the marriage such as sharing homes with parents or undertaking unrealistic financial obligations in order to secure a home of one's own.

None of these reasons is unique to Hungary. Marriage the world over is confronted by such difficulties, challenges and shortcomings. What makes Hungary of interest is that it has always had a high divorce rate, even before the Second World War, and its legislators have made the process of obtaining a divorce an even more straightforward one based simply on the complete and irretrievable breakdown of the marriage.

All the talk of women as wage-earners and two-job families, and the importance of taking the needs of the children involved in a divorce into account, can sometimes give the impression that divorce as a social problem has been solved. Yet the fact remains that most women do not work full-time and even when they do they do not, as we have seen in Chapter 3, earn as much as their husbands. And most women end up with the custody of their children. And many women find it extremely difficult to manage the one-parent situation. And divorced men find it very much easier to remarry than do divorced women.

Indeed, social concern regarding divorce could be reduced to consideration of two main issues – the problem of the one-parent family and the related but separate issue of the emotional impact on the psychological health and development of the children of divorced parents. In Britain, one-parent families now make up one in eight of all families with children. Since 1971, the overwhelming majority of one-parent families have consistently been headed by women. A decade ago, lone mothers were just as likely to be employed as married mothers but there has been a massive reduction in the proportion of lone mothers in employment in the last few years. Even in 1981, when more single-parent mothers were employed, half were living at or below the poverty line and in 1982 they were twice as likely to have incomes in the bottom fifth of the income distribution as couples with children. On the basis of several sources, the Family Policy Studies Centre has estimated that one-parent families currently number between 900,000 and 1 million, and include at least 1½ million children.

Of course, many divorced single parents remarry: it has been estimated that 80 per cent of those divorcing under the age of thirty will remarry within five years. Divorced women with children under ten years of age are the most likely to remarry. But the fact remains that for a substantial number of divorced parents with custody of children, the overwhelming majority of whom are women, financial difficulties are ubiquitous. This fact is compounded by the association between low social class and divorce, at least in Britain. There is a widespread myth to the effect that divorce is a middle-class phenomenon whereas in fact the highest rates are to be found in social class V (unskilled manual workers).

Estimating the effects on children of marital breakdown is not easy yet it is not exactly an academic question, given that on present trends approximately 20 per cent of the children born in the 1970s are going to experience a parental divorce. Such figures are often cited by opponents of divorce as representing an unparalleled level of family dissolution, but it needs to be remembered that in the past mortality of parents during the child-rearing years was very much higher than today and loss by death may have been more common than today's rates of marital separation. American data, summarised by Martin Richards and Margaret Dyson of the Child Care and Development Group at the University of Cambridge, suggest that marital disruption was more common at the turn of the century than in the 1960s (when divorce rates in America were rather higher than those in Britain today).

Having said that, research findings suggest that there is a wide difference in the responses of children to the death of a parent and a marital separation. The effects of the latter are not only more long-lasting and severe for children but there are qualitative differences. Such differences are illustrated by one American study which showed that American teenage girls from separated families spent more time with boys and were more attention-seeking compared with those from families where the parents remained married, while the children of widows were shy and retiring. Anti-social behaviour is much more likely to be seen in teenagers from separated families than in those from families where one parent has died.

In the review by Richards and Dyson of the literature on separation, divorce and child development they systematically examine the research data relating to the responses of pre-school children, of those between school age and puberty, and of adolescents. They also examine the effects of step-parenting and remarriage in terms of whether they ameliorate or aggravate some of the adverse effects of divorce. They often point out, however, that good research evidence is either very incomplete or totally lacking.

Nevertheless, they conclude that marital separation is a process with profound consequences for children. The most common reactions are anger, directed at one or both parents, sadness and depression. An important factor in how children cope with their parents' separation is the degree of withdrawal of parental emotional support and involvement. This is frequent at separation due to the parents being themselves distressed and not infrequently depressed. Effects on social behaviour and schoolwork may persist through childhood if the separation occurs in the early years but much depends on the situation after the parents have separated.

> In general, a good relationship with both parents seems to be protective while problems may be exacerbated by the falling living standards that usually follow separation, or by the remarriage of the parents. In many matters, such as remarriage, the evidence is too incomplete to provide the basis for constructive advice. While we have found no evidence that remarriage is beneficial to children we know little about the probably differing effects of various remarriage situations.[1]

For example, is continuing contact with a separated father protective against the stress of maternal remarriage? What, if any, are the consequences of the step-parent bringing his or her own children into the household? There is some evidence that parental remarriage, often encouraged 'for the sake of the children', may actually be more damaging than being part of a good one-parent family.

Qualifying all these comments is the fact that until relatively recently much of this work has been American in origin and the

SOME FAMILY INDICATORS IN EUROPE*										
	IRELAND	UK	FRANCE	BELGIUM	NETHERLANDS	LUXEMBOURG	DENMARK	WEST GERMANY	ITALY	GREECE
AVERAGE AGE OF WOMAN AT BIRTH OF FIRST CHILD	24·9	25·0	25·0	24·5	25·7	n/a	24·8	25·2	24·9	23·3
ONE-PARENT FAMILIES AS % OF ALL FAMILIES	5·6	11·9	10·2	9·8	10·7	13·3	12·0	9·1	9·4	n/a
ILLEGITIMATE BIRTHS PER 100 LIVE BIRTHS	5·4	12·5	12·7	3·4	4·8	7·1	35·8	7·9	4·3	1·6
PROPORTION OF FEMALES IN THE TOTAL WORKING POPULATION	28·3	39·1	39·3	38·1	33·4	29·9	44·9	38·2	33·6	n/a
*FAMILY POLICY STUDIES CENTRE, LONDON, 1984										

tradition and pattern of such an area of study is only now spreading to Europe.

What is clear is that divorce and separation contribute to ill-health in the adult participants. High rates of anxiety, depression, irritability, tension and mood swings are reported in separated and divorced men and women. Studies in British general practice show that marital problems head the list of complaints for women presenting with symptoms of anxiety and depression, while such problems come second after employment difficulties for men. Marital disharmony, breakdown and divorce are positively associated with severe depressive illness, attempted suicide and suicide itself.

Such evidence all goes to support the notion of divorce as a 'social problem'. At the present time, my own country of Ireland has firmly opposed altering the constitution and making divorce legal. The Irish debate revolved around the familiar issues of the plight of the one-parent family, the impact on children and the claim that easy divorce in some way cheapens marriage, removes the strength which married couples derive from the wider social and cultural disapproval of legally-approved marital dissolution.

It is doubtful, however, that a cheapening of the ideal of marriage has either contributed to or been produced by the provision of easier forms of divorce. Everywhere one looks, one encounters highly idealised and highly demanding expectations of what marriage as an institution can provide. It is precisely because marriage is so revered that it breaks down so frequently.

There are clearly ways of limiting the destructive and damaging effects of divorce but it is difficult to see how they can be implemented without a fairly thorough reassessment of the way we think about marriage and the family and the way we currently support both. That takes us to the next chapter.

7 TOWARDS THE NEW LOVELAWS

In the face of the many cultural and social differences which appear to affect the way that personal relationships are organised and regulated around the world, it is surprising the extent to which the central issues remain stubbornly the same. Virtually everywhere now, young people are exhorted to postpone marriage until they are well into their twenties. At the same time, however, we hark back to seemingly halcyon days when premarital sexuality was unknown (or at least not talked about), brides approached the altar appropriately dressed in virginal white, illegitimacy was a scandal, and good girls simply said no. Couples are now urged to decide for themselves whether and when to have children. Yet few societies seem willing to provide the family with much political and social support and in the more affluent ones children now compete for existence against luxury items such as glamorous holidays and video equipment. Marriage is portrayed less as a social institution and legal contract than as a means to self-discovery, the expression of an effort to make life a fuller experience, a touchstone of the quality of human existence; at the same time, it has acquired a fragility and brittleness which render it more vulnerable to stresses and strains than at any time in its history.

Attempts to come to terms with such expectations, strains and contradictions appear fraught with difficulty. Not the least is the tendency, in Britain at least, to appeal to a consensus concerning personal relationships which no longer exists, if indeed it ever did. It is often argued that in this age of mass communications and the so-called global village, people are becoming more and more alike. There is, it is said, widespread uniformity and conformity. In the area of personal and sexual relationships I doubt if this is true. A combination of affluence, social mobility and immigration has resulted in a Britain not of consensus but of minorities. Increasingly, if somewhat unwillingly, the rights of numerous minorities, ethnic, regional, religious, generational and sexual, are being acknowledged as legitimate. One consequence is that even if it were more desirable to arrive at a national consensus on such matters as teenage sexual behaviour, cohabitation, premarital intercourse, contraception, abortion, sex roles in marriage, divorce, it is no longer possible. In the light of this lack of a genuine consensus, this final chapter considers a number of issues raised in earlier parts of this book.

Teenage Sexuality

Between the policy of segregation of the teenage sexes in southern India and the untrammelled liberty of adolescents in southern California, is there a middle way? If our teenagers are to avoid committing themselves to marriage before they have completed education and training and if, simultaneously, they are to avoid pregnancy and abortion, what are they supposed to do with their sexual desires, their need for intimacy, their romantic feelings? Chastity, the traditionalists robustly reply. Sex education coupled with contraceptive advice and availability, is the somewhat more uneasy liberal response. All of this, plus the widespread and easy availability of abortion facilities, insist the determined sexual radicals.

In practice, of course, the British response is a classic fudge. Sex education is chaotic in that there is not even agreement as to what it should consist of and who should administer it. I sit on the Health Education Council of England and Wales and can testify to the fact that there is no subject of more delicacy and political sensitivity, no topic which causes a more worried flurry of unease and consternation amongst the Council's members and the government advisers than any discussion of what the Council is doing or intends to do about sex education. While most people appear to agree that teenagers should know the facts of life, there is little agreement on anything else. For some, the main point of passing on sexual knowledge is as a deterrent: an emphasis on venereal disease, unwanted pregnancy and the horrors of teenage abortion is justified on the grounds that something has to keep the damnable hormonal urges in check. Such an approach emphasises the immaturity of teenagers and the view that not only marriage but sex itself

*A young boy learns
about the facts of life
at school*

should wait for intellectual maturity to catch up with biological
maturity. A more positive emphasis, laying stress on the factual
aspects of sexuality, and providing information not merely
about sexual intercourse but about sexual techniques, mastur-
bation, contraception, abortion and homosexuality, lays itself
open to accusations of exploring techniques but not feelings,
giving a sort of car maintenance guide to the facts of life.
Virtually everyone wants a humane, rounded, comprehensive
form of sex education involving the psychological and social
aspects of personal relationships as well as their biological
bases, but attempts to provide such a framework run the risk of
seeming to encourage young people to taste the joys of the forbidden fruit.

What is undeniable is the lengthy delay between biological
maturity and marriage in modern societies. The menarche for
British girls is about thirteen years of age. British boys experience their first ejaculation on average a year or two later. The

median age for marriage in the UK is about twenty-five for men and twenty-three for women. That is to say, at least a decade elapses between biological maturation and marriage. The 1984 British MORI poll suggested that only 10 per cent of British youth were still virgins by the age of twenty-five whereas 25 per cent had had sexual experience by their seventeenth birthday. In this respect, they differ little from their contemporaries in most other Western European countries. In a 1981 report on sex education and adolescence in Europe, the Polish sociologist, Mikotaj Kozakiewicz, reported that most young people considered premarital intercourse acceptable, even desirable. Even in such traditionally Catholic countries as Poland and Ireland, it is only a minority of young people who unreservedly condemn premarital sexual experience. The same report questioned the tendency to equate teenage sexual experience with promiscuity. The young people surveyed clearly viewed sexuality primarily as an expression of feelings of love. Approval was highest for premarital intercourse between engaged couples. It was lower, though still high, for sex between lovers but fell away sharply when sexual intercourse between casual acquaintances was considered.

How does Britain fare? Not very well, it has to be said. If we take abortion, then in 1982 just over 32 per cent of teenage conceptions in England and Wales were terminated by abortion, the proportion having risen from just over 21 per cent in 1971. In 1984, there were just under 170,000 abortions in England and Wales, an increase of 4·8 per cent over the preceding year. But the abortion rate for teenagers was up *that* year by 7 per cent.

Compare Britain with Sweden, a country so often portrayed by right-wing critics as a haven of unrestricted if dour sexual activity. Abortion there has been available on demand since 1975. This entitles the woman herself to decide up to the eighteenth week whether or not to complete her pregnancy. But since 1975 there has been a steady *fall* in teenage abortions in Sweden of 25 per cent over the period. It is also worth noting that whereas in Sweden 90 per cent of all abortions are undertaken not later than the twelfth week of pregnancy, one in six of all abortions in England and Wales in 1984 involved pregnancies of twelve or more weeks' duration and almost 6000, or 3·5 per cent, were undertaken after eighteen weeks.

The Swedes have since 1974 taken a characteristically forthright attitude towards sex education. All essential facts about sex are included and teaching begins not with plant and animal reproduction but with human reproduction. It starts in the first primary school year and continues throughout school life. Where formerly sexual intercourse was discussed only in the context of marriage, suggesting that sex outside marriage was improper, the fourth edition of a Swedish teacher's manual, *Teaching on Sexual and Personal Relationships*, which appeared in 1974, makes it clear that it should be dealt with separately since, 'It is self-evident to most Swedes that a premarital sexual relationship between people who have an intimate personal relationship and who display concern and responsibility towards each other, is entirely proper.'

It is probably self-evident to most Britons too but to date there has been a much greater reluctance to express such explicit views in public. Motives for sexual abstinence prior to marriage include,

1 The value of 'saving' oneself for marriage alone
2 The parallel between the maturity of love and its bodily expression
3 The responsibility for one's partner and for possible pregnancy
4 The view that ideal or 'perfect' intercourse only occurs in marriage.

Modern Church interpretations of such concepts as 'purity' and 'chastity', however, are somewhat more complex than at first might appear. There are signs, particularly in the statements of some European theologians, of a desire to accommodate those Catholic moralists who speak in favour of the optional nature of premarital intercourse between engaged couples if it is an expression of mutual love and responsibility.

If premarital chastity is not then to be an absolute value, what stands between its abandonment and such unwanted consequences as abortion or illegitimacy? Sex education on its own will not ensure that young people do not become pregnant. Like Sweden, the Netherlands has an energetic policy on sex education. Yet a survey in 1981[1] revealed that no contraceptive measures were taken by either partner in 26% of the cases of teenage sexual intercourse – a fact reflected in the comparatively high abortion rates for this age group.

What of a country which appears to take premarital chastity very seriously indeed? In the Irish Republic illegitimacy is comparatively low. Abortion is virtually non-existent, given the highly restrictive abortion laws there. Yet teenage sexuality can hardly be described as tamed. While the country has the lowest rate of induced abortions in Europe, it has the highest figures of infanticide, 655 in 1975. In that year there were 1966 cases where the birth of a child was kept secret, and 983 infants were abandoned. Moreover, it has recently been estimated that annually some 4000 induced abortions are performed on Irish women who come to the UK to avail themselves of the liberal abortion laws there; among these, single mothers account for 80 per cent, and 50 per cent of these are under twenty-five.

The unavoidable conclusion, it would appear, is that if we seriously wish to minimise the greatest evils that result from demanding a ten-year moratorium on marriage following biological maturation, then we must consider implementing:

1 A thorough, comprehensive and evaluated programme of sex education involving young people, parents, teachers and others concerned with the moral, physical and psychological welfare of young people

2 A linked programme of education concerning child-bearing, child-rearing and marriage

3 A programme of contraceptive advice backed up by the appropriate provision of contraceptives and involving both men and women

4 A campaign aimed at highlighting the adverse physical, psychological and social consequences of teenage pregnancy and abortion, and at reducing teenage abortion rates specifically

5 A discussion in society at large concerning the bases on which premarital sexual relationships are conducted.

Teenage sexual activity has always been with us but we are now circumscribing it with contradictory customs and controls. In an increasingly eroticised society we are encouraging young people to defer marriage. We are ambivalent about postponing sexual intercourse. We are even more ambivalent about the wisdom of providing full, frank sex education and most ambivalent of all about contraception. We do not seem to know quite what to do with teenage sexuality and our confusion shows in the varying rates of illegitimacy, abortion and sexually transmitted diseases in this age group around the world.

Cohabitation

If teenage sexual activity is often portrayed as promiscuity, the growing custom of cohabitation is likewise seen as an indication that young people no longer take marriage seriously and that the so-called 'cereal-packet norm' of the family (consisting of a mother, a father and their two children) is on the way out. As we saw in Chapter 2, however, there is little evidence that marriage is losing its appeal, but in Britain cohabitation is increasing rapidly. For example, only 3 per cent of women who married for the first time in the late 1960s had lived with their husbands before they were married. By the early 1970s this had risen to 10 per cent and by the late 1970s the proportion was 20 per cent. At that time, one in ten single women aged between twenty and twenty-nine were reported as currently cohabiting. What was unacceptable a generation ago has become much more the custom despite the unease often felt by the parents of those involved. It seems highly likely that cohabitation will be commonplace by the turn of the century.

In Sweden and Denmark the trend is particularly marked. A Danish report, commenting on the findings of a survey conducted in 1978 among four groups of people, all aged between eighteen and fifty (those divorced in 1972, those married in 1972, those married for at least ten years, and single people), showed that 27 per cent of the single people but also 34 per cent of the divorced people were cohabiting. A total of 35 per cent of people living together had been doing so for at least two years and 20 per cent of these for more than three years.

To some observers, such as Jean Morsa of the Centre d'Étude de la Population et de la Famille in Brussels, cohabitation, particularly when it is accompanied by illegitimate births, is throwing marriage into disarray and is causing the collapse or breakdown of the traditional family. It is certainly true that long-term cohabitation is proving compatible with the birth of children and it is this development which marks contemporary cohabitation as different from its historical predecessors. The acceptance in Sweden and Denmark of what were traditionally considered to be illegitimate births and the apparent absence of social pressure to restrict them are sure signs, in Morsa's view, 'of a radical change in Swedish and Danish society'.

However, in Sweden and Denmark, as in America, Britain, Germany and France, most of the people who live together do eventually get married. In Sweden it is now common for a man and a woman to move in together, have one or two children and finally marry. Some 37 per cent of all Swedish infants are born to unwed parents. Provided the father acknowledges his parenthood, the child has exactly the same rights, including those of inheritance, as does a child born within marriage.

And yet, despite the fact that officially marriage is seen as just another form of cohabitation, Swedish marriage survives — although the Swedish divorce rate is high. Studies there indicate that despite a profound tolerance of cohabitation as a relationship in which to have children, there is agreement that in various ways legal marriage is 'more secure' and indicates more 'sincerity of involvement'. Most significant is the fact that the majority of cohabitants intend to marry some day.

So is the traditional family under threat? A much-quoted statistic is the one that states that the so-called typical family of a married couple with the father in full-time employment and the mother at home, and with two dependent children, is not typical at all but represents only one household in twenty at any one point in time. However, what this simple statistic conceals is the fact that a substantial proportion of families will pass through this stage at some point in their lives and that more than 80 per cent of Britain's 11 million children live with both their natural parents. The 'typical' traditional family is still alive and reasonably healthy, although a combination of trends, which include the growing involvement by women in work outside the home, a smaller family size and a steady rise in divorce, has greatly altered its nature and life history.

As the family changes in size, it may well be changing in other ways too. For example, it does appear that the traditional, extended family emphasised, both explicitly and implicitly, the collective interests of the group and relegated the personal needs and ambitions of individual members to second place. It was the family as a group which guaranteed its members a social existence. In such a traditional group, each member contributed to the best of his or her ability to the achievement of the collective aims. Such a model also implied a close-knit, mutual support. As the alliance between families which traditional marriage forged meant that the marriage itself was rendered virtually indissoluble, personal aims being once more subjugated to the needs of the group, so the traditional family, through its separate but interlocking roles, created a sense of security and interdependence among its members. It was precisely because the traditional father and mother did not do the same jobs, did not undertake the same roles that each depended on the other. Even the common method of birth control in the pre-pill era, coitus interruptus, demanded self-denial and was not practised primarily for personal ends.

The shrinking of the traditional family and the economic and political circumstances which have brought it about favour the single-child or the two-child family. Such children, together with their parents, are encouraged to seek self-fulfilment. Leisure, once seen as idleness, is reinterpreted as an excellent opportunity for personal enrichment, development and culture. And Morsa believes that the family now takes second place to the fulfilment of the aims of its members.

> Indeed, the family is formed because the plans and aspirations of the spouses appear to coincide. This is the mark of its precariousness; it only needs one of them to find that in fact the coincidence was imaginary or that it has disappeared, and the marriage breaks up. Each partner brings to the marriage his or her understanding, personality and attentiveness to the other. He or she need only find that the enrichment expected in return is not being received and the family breaks up.[2]

One of the more recent pressures within the family is that which demands a greater equality of roles for wife and husband, father and mother. Wives who have gone out to work have discovered that while it gives them liberty, satisfaction, money and independence, it does not necessarily give them equality. Low levels of unionisation, the vulnerability of the part-time worker, sex discrimination in the labour market and discriminatory employment and redundancy policies are just some of the problems women face outside the home. But within it too, as we saw in Chapter 3, the roles appear unequal. In turn, this has led to a call for the emergence of a new man.

The New Man

Enough of the talk about raising women's consciousness and the need for female revolution, cry today's feminists, it is not women who have to change, it is men. The new man, it turns out, is one who embodies virtues which characteristically have hitherto been deemed to be feminine. But the new man is not effeminate. Gentleness, sensitivity, a lack of aggression, a sense of proportion are some of the qualities of the new man. But the new man is not weak. Rather he is a macho househusband, capable of taking over the domestic cleaning, of feeding junior, of caring for sick children and animals and not merely able to undertake the do-it-yourself manly chores preferred by his unliberated counterpart. And, inevitably it would seem, the new man is Swedish.

In Sweden, virtually all women work until the birth of their child and more and more return to work within the first postpartum year. The number of full-time housewives has fallen sharply, from 26 per cent in 1979 to 12 per cent in 1984. To ensure true equality of employment, not merely outside the home but within it too, the Swedes have pioneered a number of pieces of social legislation. One involves the provision of parental insurance by means of which the parents are entitled to divide leave of absence for child-rearing reasons between them. This insurance replaced the earlier maternity insurance scheme, thus demonstrating that child care is the concern of fathers as well as mothers. The parental insurance law entitles parents to leave of absence in connection with childbirth and for purposes of child care. Parents are entitled to take turns in staying at home with their new-born children for a period of 270 days and the stay-at-home parent receives compensation for loss of earnings. Consequently, the majority of families do not lose anything economically by the best-paid parent, usually the father, staying at home. Parents are entitled to another ninety days' leave of absence but only at a standard benefit rate. This benefit is also payable to students and to full-time housewives.

All Swedish fathers are entitled to ten days' leave of absence with loss of earnings compensation in connection with each childbirth. Parents are also entitled to loss of earnings compensation when they stay at home to look after a sick child. This entitlement comprises up to sixty days' leave per child each year. Under the terms of a related scheme, parents of pre-school children are entitled to a six-hour working day without, however, compensation for loss of earnings.

The entire scheme has been expanded since its introduction. Nearly all fathers (85 per cent) take time off in connection with childbirth but only one in five takes time off in order to look after his baby. On average, fathers stay at home for only forty-one days during the first eighteen months of the child's life. On the other hand, men extensively avail themselves of the opportunity of staying at home to look after sick children. Indeed they do so almost to the same extent as mothers, namely seven days per annum. It is less common for male industrial workers to take parental leave than it is for local and national government officials. At mixed workplaces, the general climate is more favourably disposed towards men taking parental leave.

This new pattern of life which has evolved in Sweden since the 1960s has caused attention to focus on the question of shorter working hours. It has been the women's organisations which have pressed the demand for a significant reduction in daily working hours, the aim being a six-hour day. In a society where all adults are gainfully employed, both women and men, so the argument goes, must have time for what is commonly termed the reproductive part of life – the provision of care and attention for children and relatives, for the home and for one's private life. A full working day in line with a normal forty-hour working week, the argument presses on, is too much for families with children. Without further social engineering, this produces a society in which there is a segregated labour market with men working full-time and overtime and women working part-time. The best way of achieving equalisation of men's and women's working hours, the women's organisations insist, is by a radical reduction of the working hours.

For several years during the early 1970s, political parties and the trades unions were supportive but the economic downturn in the 1980s took some of the impetus away. Yet today 71 per cent of Swedish women and 62 per cent of Swedish men would prefer shorter hours to higher pay while a substantial minority, 18 per cent of men and 26 per cent of women, would even be prepared to accept shorter working hours with a corresponding reduction of pay.

Manipulating the hours that men and women work, restructuring the employment system so that men can take paternity leave, may well seem a somewhat excessive way of persuading men to do a little more of the washing up. Some men are frankly contemptuous but they leave themselves open to the allegation, made most pointedly by Marilyn French, to the effect that, 'One can touch the depths of male contempt for femaleness by suggesting that a man act like a woman or consider himself one'. The dilemma has been that in pursuit of sexual and social equality, women have had to accept a male world with its emphasis on power, status, achievement and control. The most successful women in such a world often seem little more than surrogate males.

But it remains a male world in Sweden for all these ingenious efforts. It is indeed true that many men have begun to discover new sides of themselves, new needs, new desires. One consequence has been that some have chosen to 'drop out' and turn their backs on a career. In the past few years, several politicians have made dramatic exits from public life, explaining that they wanted more time for themselves and their families and that a political career made a normal family life virtually impossible. Constant lack of time is a serious problem for parents who have full-time employment. Commenting on this central issue, the authors of *Side by Side*, a report on equality between the sexes in Sweden presented to the Nairobi Conference on Women, observed forcefully,

> To be together with one's children is also work, requiring thought and concentration, insight and creativity. We talk all too little about how wonderful parenthood can be. Instead, for many parents, children have become an obstacle, a baby-sitting problem. There are, however, parents who take the opposite view, that it is the job which deprives them of the opportunity to follow the development of their own children.[3]

The new man, therefore, wants more time for life within the home, the new woman more time for life outside it. How much equality should there be? In the 1985 British Social Attitudes Survey, wives were generally satisfied with the amount of work at home their husbands did (although 20 per cent thought their husbands should do more) while most husbands thought they did just about the right amount of work at home (though again 20 per cent admitted they could do more). While this survey found that both men and women favoured a more equal division of labour than existed, the answers from both sexes were still far from egalitarian. Ideals were tempered by current experience and it is clear that married men and women were less egalitarian in their replies than either the formerly married or the never married. But the survey did find that those aged between eighteen and twenty-four were 'much more egalitarian than the general population'. However, analysis revealed that it was not so much youth as being unmarried which explained this egalitarianism. There was a high proportion of unmarried individuals in the eighteen to twenty-four group; the answers from the married eighteen- to twenty-four-year-olds were 'not dissimilar to that of the general population'.

The Family Policy Studies Unit, commenting on the findings of the British Social Attitudes Survey, concluded that the picture is 'depressingly inegalitarian'. Even more gloomy is the remark made by the report's editors, G. Airey and R. Jowell, to the effect that, 'It is also probably similar to the pattern that could have been produced if we had asked the same questions in Britain at any time during the past thirty years or so.'

It is not merely the practical aspects of home care that are seen to be particularly 'feminine' tasks. The emotional aspects of child care are more likely to be the working woman's responsibility than the working man's. Over and over again, in countries as seemingly progressive as Sweden, the Netherlands and America, full-time working women end up putting substantial hours into looking after the home, the children, even the au pair, domestic help or nanny if there is one. Clearly the creation of the new man is taking time. There are signs that by the time he is created there may not be all that many children on whom he can demonstrate his new-found qualities.

Children: To Have or Have Not
Since 1965 there has been a steady decline in fertility in most Western European countries. Among the generation born in 1954, the proportion of women destined to remain childless is

likely to be about 22 per cent in West Germany, 21 per cent in England and Wales, 20 per cent in Switzerland and 11 per cent in France. In some countries, such as Austria and the Netherlands, it could exceed 25 per cent.

In West Germany, there is growing concern. 'Sterben die Deutschen aus?' is the question asked. (Will the Germans become extinct?) The population is declining by 0·3 per cent per year. If the tendency for German couples to have no children or only one child were to continue, the population of the Federal Republic would fall from around 61 million today to 38 million by the year 2035. As it is, many kindergartens are being closed. Elementary schools have fewer children and teachers have a relatively high level of unemployment. Even producers of baby food have been hit and are feverishly switching their products to those catering for old people, of whom there are increasing numbers. The most immediate impact is on the West German Army and there are predictions that by the late 1980s the size of the standing army will have to be drastically cut.

Germany's population reached its peak in 1973 when it stood at 61·9 million. In 1985 it stood at 61·035. But the fall has been even steeper. There are many more immigrants in the country than there were in 1973 and the indigenous German population is now estimated at only 56 million. The country's birth rate, for some time the lowest in the world, is now so flat that three West Germans die for every two that are born. Does it much matter, however, that West Germany faces a steady population decline? After all, the world in general faces a population crisis of quite different proportions. Demographers admit frankly that they find it difficult to make predictions about falling populations; they have had so little practice. But there are worries, most notably economic ones. By the year 2030, according to one German prediction, each individual in work will effectively be supporting one retired individual, badly straining the country's generous pension arrangements. At the present time, German workers contribute 19 per cent of their wages to maintain pension funds. Economists predict that an upper limit of 25 per cent as a contribution may just work. If the German population does decline to the predicted level of 38 million, the proportion will have to rise to a staggering 35 per cent.

At a time of chronic unemployment it may seem particularly

perverse to talk of labour shortages yet these too may be a serious problem. But it is the increase in the proportion of economically inactive people which seems likely to pose the greatest difficulty. While medical progress has helped many people to live to a ripe old age, technological progress has effectively excluded most of them from the production system at an ever younger age. There is also the question of whether there are subtle yet significant effects on the vitality of a nation exercised by a slow, steady decline in the proportion of its people that are youthful and an equivalent remorseless rise in the proportion of those who are not?

But why have some of the most affluent countries in Europe seemingly lost the will or the interest to replace themselves? Sociologists blame the oral contraceptive pill, the desire of more women to develop full-time careers and the growing egocentric urge to enjoy leisure activities unfettered by the duties of parenthood. In one German study, a psychologist, Guenther Opitz, found that only 10 per cent of ninety-three couples born after the Second World War believed that children were more important than consumer goods or careers. The majority of his respondents fell into categories he tellingly labelled as 'dynamic globe-trotters', 'prestige-minded consumers' and '*petit bourgeois* home builders' who usually want no more than one child, if indeed any at all.

Another cause, cited in a German government report, is an allegedly abiding disdain towards children whose noisy habits may jar the German penchant for neatness and order. For example, many newspaper advertisements listing apartments for rent in West German cities specify that no children are allowed, whereas dogs are usually tolerated. The letters editor of *Eltern* (*Parents*) magazine is quoted as saying that children are themselves thought of as luxury goods which you have to plan for in great detail as you would plan for a car or a washing-machine. They do indeed provide emotional satisfaction – but they must not get in the way. This has been termed the 'ghetto attitude' to children; they are all right in schools and inside the house and in special places such as the puppet theatre but elsewhere they are a nuisance and to be discouraged.

The government's reaction has been to improve child-care facilities, parental-leave terms and, by means of special payments, to try to attract unmarried pregnant women away from abortion clinics. But there is little evidence that Germans avoid having children because they lack the financial means to provide for them. One German research group, unimpressed by the reasons for Germany's spectacular population decline, studied 700 couples for a period of three years. The couples, apart from the fact that they all lived in Bavaria, were representative of West German society as a whole in terms of their most important socio-demographic characteristics. The majority of these couples did express the wish to have children but there was no evidence of any frustrated desire to have large families. (The West German Chancellor, in a widely publicised speech in 1983, asserted that many couples would like to have more children but financial considerations prevented them.) Those women who expressed firm views about not having children certainly stuck to their decision throughout the three years of the study. Children were seen not to be compatible with wealth, free time and women working whereas the decision to have them appeared influenced by religious values, by the desire of one or other partner to have a child and by the notion of 'emotional support in old age'.

One of the most interesting findings was that which revealed the negative attitude of German society to children. The more children the couples sampled had, the more hostile and negative their relationships were with their neighbours. Other aspects of German life, including the size and design of houses, and the attitude to children in restaurants and other public places, both reflect and shape public and personal valuation of child-bearing and rearing.

In trying to stimulate population growth through fiscal policy, the present German government reawakens sensitive echoes of the past. The Nazis, in an effort to counter the dramatic fall in the birth rate after the Depression, punished abortions and introduced cheap loans to couples; the more children they produced, the less money they would have to pay back. There were generous allowances for every child and families with more than four children could expect the State to pay for their education in full. The present West German government is considering tax concessions for families with children, maternity pay for every mother and special grants for parents who stay at home to look after the children. Yet the Swedish experience, and similar attempts to stimulate child-bearing in Hungary, suggest that the provision of even the most generous of family support systems does not appear to alter the comparative attractions of children and the material good things of life.

In Britain, financial supports are not ostensibly provided for population-boosting purposes. In recent years, while the birth rate has fallen the various family supports provided by the State have fallen too. This fact does not prevent politicians of various political hues earnestly protesting their firm commitment to the importance of family life. Child benefit in 1981 was worth less, relatively speaking, than in 1960 and was very much lower in real terms than that in 1965 and 1979. For larger, four-child families, there was a 20 per cent decline in child support in real terms between 1965 and 1981. By contrast, the net income of childless couples rose in real terms during the same period.

In so far as couples with children have managed to hold their own financially, it has been due not to State support but to a rise in the number of mothers who are going out to work. One analyst of these family financial trends, David Piachaud, believes that these trends have not been sufficiently analysed and appreciated by political and social planners.

> If mothers stay at home to care for their children, as some urge them to do, their families will experience lower living standards than those enjoyed by the childless. Child benefits do not adequately compensate for the absence of a second wage-earner. If, however, society expects both mothers and fathers to work outside the home, this has implications for nursery provision, day-care facilities and other child-care services. At present neither of these two policy implications are being faced up to. We have moved into an era of 'dual worker' families but have not thought through the policy consequences.[4]

Nor do we show much sign of thinking through today. Despite what the politicians say, the tax and child benefit system in Britain appears to favour the childless and those with the fewest children. Such a situation may well reflect a feeling in Europe that since there are too many mouths to feed throughout the world it might be better if there were less to feed in affluent Europe. It may simply reflect the fact that at the present time, the emphasis is on personal development, self-expression through work and financial independence and that child-bearing and rearing are seen as antipathetic activities. It is difficult in this regard to contest the conclusions of a Council of Europe report on fertility trends to the effect that the 'organisation of society is not adapted to allow people, and in particular women, to combine the realisation of modern-life options with the will to start a family or to bring up several children'.

It may well be that at the present time the European public is impressed with the advantages of shrinking fertility. And there are advantages. In general, for example, growing up as a child in a two-child or even a one-child family appears to exercise favourable effects on the physical and the intellectual development of children. The disappearance of the very large family, which was often characterised by higher risks of social problems, handicap and disability, particularly in socially deprived groups, is said to have had favourable effects on mental and physical health and on social performance and success. The decrease in family size has undoubtedly contributed to the emancipation of many women with respect to their personal development and financial independence. And it may very well be that with the proliferation of smaller families will come a less asymmetrical division of roles involving the two parents within the family, giving men a greater opportunity to participate in fatherhood and household activities.

However, what is unarguable is that the maintenance of the present fertility levels in most of the countries of Europe, East and West, will lead in the medium to long term to a considerable decrease in and ageing of the population. Commenting on the possible consequences of such developments, J. C. Chesnais, of the Institut National d'Études Démographiques in Paris, suggests that the growing shortage of labour (which will follow this particular period of high unemployment) will lead many countries back to a dependence on immigration. One may legitimately wonder, he asks,

> ... whether this is not one of the potential contradictions of the future; will rich, ageing and shrinking societies be able to accommodate the poor, prolific communities to which, more than any other, they may be tempted to resort in order to resolve their difficulties? Will such societies, characterised by a constant fall in the number of young persons in work, be capable of coping with the impact of increasingly keen international competition? The question is open to doubt.

What is clear is that falling fertility is yet another issue which requires that the countries of Europe undertake a profound reassessment of social policies relating to couples and their decision whether or not to have children. And such a consideration brings us full circle. Teenage sexuality, the choice of partner, the roles of wives and husbands, the decision to have children, to have lovers, to part, to divorce, to remarry – these are subjects of inordinate importance to individuals. They exude a personal, almost a private significance. What on earth have they to do with the wider community, the government, the State? Surely the way we live our personal lives is in the final resort our own business?

Up to a point the answer is clearly yes – but quite where the point is placed is arguable. In terms of the effects and the costs of teenage pregnancy, teenage abortion, teenage relationships and sexuality, the State is mightily involved. In terms of battles over property and custody and maintenance, the wider community and the State have more than a passing interest in marital breakdown and divorce. In terms of the remarkable and poorly understood ramifications of rising and falling fertility rates on the social structure and stability of society, the State has an enormous stake in the decision taken by individual couples to reproduce.

What is surprising, given this state of affairs, is the remarkably haphazard way in which governments throughout the world exercise their responsibility and manifest their interest. It is not so much a question of the State being interfering so much as reacting to pressures, trends and developments without having at any stage a very clear idea of quite how the family and marriage might be sustained and protected in a systematic way. The State, in various parts of the world, has sometimes initiated, sometimes opposed, more often than not accommodated itself to such developments as married women working. But the full implications of such a development on child care, family life and the kind of social supports necessary for such a change to be accommodated do not appear to have been considered. To this day in Britain, many of the assumptions about family life seem based on the idea of the man as the major and perhaps only breadwinner and that the typical 'worker' is a married man with a non-working wife and two children. Many British taxation and social security policies seem founded on the assumption contained in the Beveridge Report of over forty years ago, which ushered in the Welfare State, that

> all women by marriage acquire a new economic and social status, with risks and rights different from those of the unmarried. On marriage a woman gains a legal right to maintenance by her husband as a first line of defence against risks which fall directly on the solitary woman.

Such an assumption looks somewhat quaint today. Yet much of the debate focuses on the so-called nuclear family. What is needed is a family perspective within the process of policy making, a perspective which would combine a sensitivity to changing family patterns and relationships, a full recognition of family roles and functions and the monitoring and evaluation of the effects of public policy on families.

Divorce
An example of our current failure to develop and sustain such a perspective is our response to divorce. Virtually every society decries divorce, sees it as a problem and makes a show of grappling with its consequences while regretting its existence. Societies as varied as Hungary, Denmark, the United States and Britain, with high divorce rates, Egypt and Japan with low rates and Ireland and Italy where separation rather than divorce is the current response to marital breakdown all approach the subject of divorce with a disapproving eye. In such societies, the ideal of marital stability continues to be endorsed and the impact of divorce in terms of the creation of disadvantaged single-parent families, personal unhappiness and adverse psychological and behavioural consequences for the children involved is deplored.

Now such a situation is perfectly understandable. A broken marriage is, in many instances, a sad occurrence generating feelings of failure, guilt, anger and inadequacy. And we have seen, in the last chapter, some of the dire social consequences of divorce. But the fact remains that in many societies divorce has become an established fact of late twentieth-century life. In Western Europe, only a handful of societies have stood out against the trend and slowly, gradually, these countries are yielding to the remorseless pressure. As I write, the Irish Republic has just held a referendum to remove Article 41 of the

Constitution, which states that 'no law shall be enacted providing for the grant of a dissolution of marriage'. The opposition stressed the undesirable consequences of the introduction of what it sees as an attack on traditional values and culture. But a junior government minister, Mrs Nuala Fennell, put the current argument favouring divorce legislation squarely when she declared that without access to divorce

> thousands are doomed to live lonely celibate lives or alternatively join the ranks of irregular relationships within which they are discriminated against under our social welfare and tax codes, forgo legal and succession rights and have their children labelled illegitimate.

The proposed Irish legislation was modest, insisting on evidence of irretrievable breakdown and a minimum period of five years' separation. The Roman Catholic Church none the less opposed it on the grounds that once divorce is legalised every marriage is threatened, and it is not for the State to decide on the dissolubility or otherwise of marriage. The people voted against change. Contrast such a proposal with current Swedish divorce provisions where the petitioner does not have to state a reason. A couple with no children can have a divorce immediately and, if children are involved, a mere six-month cooling-off period (betänketid) is stipulated. If only one spouse wants a divorce, he or she becomes entitled to it after a six-month period.

While of course the impact of divorce on the couple warrants consideration and concern, it is the impact of divorce on any children of a breaking marriage which should preoccupy politicians and social analysts. In practice, while there is much lamentation and teeth gnashing concerning the possible dire effects of divorce, the structures which have evolved to cope with divorce and its consequences have not been the most appropriate. Although there is a substantial body of research which testifies to the fact that it is not so much divorce per se as what happens during the long-drawn-out process that leads to and follows divorce which determines whether the impact on the child is negative or not, most societies, including British society, have not drawn the obvious conclusions. In Britain, divorce remains essentially a legal process and the law, as Martin Richards has pointed out, is primarily concerned with 'the control or entry and exit from the marital state and all that flows from this in terms of such things as property rights and the legitimacy of children and the settlement of disputes that may occur at divorce.' In so far as there is consideration of the welfare of the children, it is for the most part little more than an empty gesture. The law in divorce is a blunt instrument and its adversarial quality and its emphasis on rights rather than on welfare means that in many instances the process of divorce is psychologically more damaging than it perhaps need be.

For example, the psychological evidence strongly suggests that the best interests of children are usually served if both parental relationships are maintained beyond the divorce. So one might anticipate that the divorce process would be geared towards reinforcing the continuing role of both parents. In practice, however, much divorce legislation and divorce proceedings are taken up with the issue of whom to award the custody of the child. In turn that decision is affected by the kind of evidence which each parent can marshal supporting his/her claim and denigrating the suitability of the opposing parent. It is a recipe for ensuring that divorce does indeed exact a penal psychological price, particularly for the children.

What is clearly required is some form of family court and conciliation service aimed, not primarily at reconciling warring couples, although that might on occasion occur, but at ensuring that parents and children receive support and the opportunity to discuss their feelings with a sympathetic yet detached person. There are of course agencies which provide such an opportunity – the Marriage Guidance Council and the Citizens' Advice Bureau for example – as well as individuals such as general practitioners, social workers and good friends. But it is not an intrinsic part of the divorce system and society makes no clear-cut, unequivocal and public attempt to ensure that the emotional cost of divorce is reduced to the minimum by, for example, insisting that joint custody arrangements might become the norm. There is much discussion concerning the possibility of new legislation in Britain to take account of such needs but it is interesting to note that the chances of such legislation being enacted are regarded as poor on the grounds that the cost might be excessive! The principle is conceded. The need is accepted. The enormous advantages of defusing divorce are recognised. But the fact remains that yet again a personal

A POLICY AGENDA ON FAMILIES FOR THE 1980s AND 1990s

1 *Values and Social Policy: What are the major values in relation to family life that should determine social policy?*

2 *Work and the Family: Are there steps that should be taken to enable families to meet their work and home responsibilities better, particularly those relating to the care of children and other dependants?*

3 *Family Incomes: Does the current state of family income support call for a fundamental reform – involving the integration of benefits and taxation – or can defects be tackled in a different way?*

4 *Dependency: What are the implications of changing family patterns and employment trends, and changes in the levels and nature of dependency for social security and taxation policy?*

5 *Care of Children: In providing care for the under-fives, where does the balance of responsibility lie between the family and the State? Should priority be given to providing more public resources for services and/or benefits in this area?*

6 *Care of Elderly People: What steps should be taken to build a positive partnership between the family and the State to enable an increasing number of frail, elderly people to be cared for properly?*

7 *Divorce: What are the major policy implications of the increasing divorce rate? In particular, are there measures which should be taken in relation to conciliation, financial consequences and prevention?*

8 *One-Parent Families: Given the increase in the number of one-parent families, are there specific policies required – services or benefits – to avoid hardship or distress?*

9 *The Family Process: How should a family perspective be encouraged within the policy making process? Are there mechanisms that need to be introduced in order to ensure this, such as family impact statements and a family policy review?*

Families in the Future, Study Commission on the Family, London, 1983

aspect of life, divorce, takes its lowly place in the queue behind the cost of aircraft carriers and the provision of roads because the public agenda still fails to reflect adequately private, individual concerns. And this failure persists despite the very obvious social and economic costs that divorce clearly exacts.

The Future

The Study Commission on the Family has for some years campaigned to raise the issue of personal and family life higher on the public agenda. In its final report, published in 1983, it raised a series of questions which, it argued, should constitute a policy agenda on families for the 1980s and 1990s. (See p. 191.) These questions echo those raised by *Lovelaw* in its examination of personal and social relations, laws and customs around the world. They reflect contemporary problems and possibilities inherent in personal life as the century draws to a close. They are undoubtedly amongst the issues which ordinary people debate to a far greater extent than many of the political issues and questions which receive so much time and attention at the hands of the media. Any society which believes itself to be concerned about its future would do well to address them.

But society is no more than the sum of its citizens. Individuals too are faced with the same questions. It does seem as if the balance between individual desires and their satisfactions on the one hand and the demands of groups, such as the family, on the other may be tilting too far in the direction of the former.

The irony is that if such a trend, welcome in so many ways, is unfettered, then the seeds it sows – a growing number of single-parent families, high rates of teenage abortion, the worrying spectre of large numbers of isolated and redundant people with no relatives to care for them and a society fuelling insufficient financial resources to support them – will almost certainly grow into new chains and restrictions, new lovelaws which will shift the balance once more. In effect, the testing time is now. What some critics in the developing world see as the selfishness, the decadence, the self-centredness of the developed world may well prove to be just that within the next fifty years. Or we may instead prove worthy of the freedom we so energetically pursue.

NOTES

Chapter 1

1 Debbie Taylor. In *Women: A World Report*. A New Internationalist book. Methuen, London, 1985.
2 Report of the UN Secretary General to the World Conference to Review and Appraise the Achievements of the United Nations Decade for Women: Equality, Development and Peace. Part Two. Development in Sectoral Areas. 1985.
3 *Comparative Study of Adolescent Pregnancy and Childbearing in Developed Countries*. Study Director: Elise F. Jones. Alan Guttmacher Institute, New York, 1985.
4 Dr Samuel Gatere. Lecture to secondary school students, the Alliance High School, Nairobi, 1985.
5 Brendan M. Walsh. 'Marriage in Ireland in the Twentieth Century.' In *Marriage in Ireland*. Edited by Art Cosgrove. College Press, Dublin, 1985.

Chapter 2

1 Sharan-Jeet Shan. *In My Own Name*. The Women's Press, London, 1985.
2 Nawal el Saadawi. *The Hidden Face of Eve*. Zed Books, London, 1980.
3 *Women: A World Report*. A New Internationalist book. Methuen, London, 1985.

Chapter 3

1 Report of the UN Secretary General to the World Conference to Review and Appraise the Achievements of the United Nations Decade for Women: Equality, Development and Peace. Part Two. Development in Sectoral Areas. 1985.
2 Keiko Higuchi. 'Changing Family Relationships.' In *The Japanese Family*. Foreign Press Center, Tokyo, 1981.
3 Samuel Coleman. *Family Planning in Japanese Society:*

Traditional Birth Control in a Modern Urban Culture. Princeton University Press, Princeton, N.J., 1983.

4 Joni Lovenduski. *The Guardian*, 14 January 1986.

5 Shushum Bhatia. In *World Health*. World Health Organisation, Geneva, 1985.

6 Peter Marris. 'Attachment and Society.' In *The Place of Attachment in Human Behaviour.* Edited by C. Murray Parkes and J. Stevenson-Hinde. Tavistock Publications, London, 1982.

Chapter 4

1 Debbie Taylor. In *Women: A World Report.* A New Internationalist book. Methuen, London, 1985.

2 Report of the UN Secretary General to the World Conference to Review and Appraise the Achievements of the United Nations Decade for Women: Equality, Development and Peace. Part Two. Development in Sectoral Areas. 1985.

3 Samuel Coleman. *Family Planning in Japanese Society: Traditional Birth Control in a Modern Urban Culture.* Princeton University Press, Princeton, N.J., 1983.

4 Samuel Coleman. In *Fujin Koron*, Tokyo, 1983.

5 Barbara Katz Rothman. 'The Products of Conception: The Social Context of Reproductive Choices.' In *Journal of Medical Ethics*, 11, 4, pp. 188–93, London, 1985.

6 Rosalind Petchesky. 'Reproductive Freedom: beyond "a woman's right to choose".' In *Signs: Journal of Women in Culture and Society*, 5, p. 674. University of Chicago Press, 1980.

7 Barbara Katz Rothman. 'The Products of Conception: The Social Context of Reproductive Choices.' In *Journal of Medical Ethics*, 11, 4, pp. 188–93, London, 1985.

8 *Family Incomes Since The War*, by David Piachaud. Occasional Paper No. 9. Study Commission on the Family, London, 1982.

Chapter 5

1 Alex Comfort. *More Joy of Sex.* Quartet Books, London, 1977.

2 Samuel Coleman. *Family Planning in Japanese Society: Traditional Birth Control in a Modern Urban Culture.* Princeton University Press, Princeton, N.J., 1983.

3 Keiko Higuchi. 'Changing Family Relationships.' In *The Japanese Family*. Foreign Press Center, Tokyo, 1981.

4 Gill Shepherd. *Responding to the Contraceptive Needs of Rural People*. A report to OXFAM, Kenya, 1984.

5 P. E. Mullen and L. H. Maack. 'Jealousy, Pathological Jealousy and Aggression.' In *Aggression and Dangerousness*, Chap. 5. Edited by D. P. Farrington and J. Gunn. John Wiley & Sons, Chichester, 1985.

Chapter 6

1 M. P. M. Richards and M. Dyson. *Separation, Divorce and the Development of Children: a Review*. Department of Health and Social Security, 1982.

Chapter 7

1 *Women on the Move* by Els van der Wal. Based on a study by Corrine Oudijk. Social and Cultural Planning Bureau, Rijswijk, The Hague, Netherlands, 1985.

2 Jean Morsa. *Family Formation and Dissolution: Family Structures*. Proceedings of the European Population Conference, 1982. Published in 1983 by the Council of Europe.

3 *Side by Side: A Report on Equality Between Men and Women in Sweden*. Edited by Ylva Ericsson and Ranveig Jacobsson. Ministry of Labour, Stockholm, 1985.

4 *Family Incomes Since The War*, by David Piachaud. Occasional Paper No. 9. Study Commission on the Family, London, 1982.

PICTURE CREDITS

INDEX